D1490775

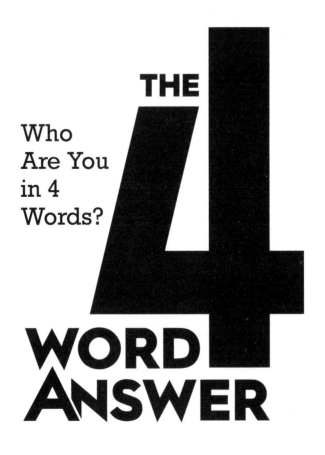

THE

Who
Are You
in 4
Words?

4

WORD ANSWER

ROB SHUTER

Post Hill
PRESS

A POST HILL PRESS BOOK
ISBN: 978-1-63758-022-6
ISBN (eBook): 978-1-63758-023-3

The 4 Word Answer:
Who Are You in 4 Words?
© 2021 by Rob Shuter
All Rights Reserved

Cover art by Cody Corcoran
Editing by Helene Harris

Post Hill Press
New York • Nashville
posthillpress.com

Published in the United States of America
1 2 3 4 5 6 7 8 9 10

Table of Contents

Chapter 1   The 4 Word Answer 1

Chapter 2   Who Are You In Four Words? 13

Chapter 3   You Is Kind! 25

Chapter 4   You Is Smart! 55

Chapter 5   You Is Important! 81

Chapter 6   You Is...(insert your name)! 123

Chapter 7   The Answer Was Just Four Words Away
             All Along 167

About the Author 181

C
H
A
P
T
E
R

The 4 Word Answer

CHANGE YOUR LIFE WITH JUST FOUR SIMPLE WORDS. AT BEST, it sounds silly. At worst, it sounds like a scam or a trick. Maybe a stunt. *The 4 Word Answer* must be another gimmick. A scheme that would make its author rich and get them on *Oprah*!

Like you, that's exactly what I assumed at first. But I was wrong, and I should know because I created it. Writing this book didn't make me rich. Reading it did! And although I've met Oprah several times, been backstage at her show more than once, and emailed with her best friend, Gayle King, I still haven't been on her show—yet!

So, how could a simple solution to all our complicated problems be just four words away? After all, wouldn't we all know about these four little words if they did all this? Well, if you give me an hour or two, I will tell you the amazing true story of someone whose big dreams evaporated over time. Someone who lost their way. Someone who needed help. Someone who wanted to find answers to all their problems. Sound familiar? Good, because that someone is *you!*

Without even knowing it's happening, your life is being stripped of hope, joy, and happiness right now. To the point where, one morning, you wake up and no longer recognize the person in the mirror. The promise and potential of youth have been replaced by fear and doubt of growing older, just like Elizabeth, who once had big dreams too.

> *Hey Rob, I want to be that young, pretty girl with thick golden hair, cavorting around town, swinging my precious Kate Spade bag again. I don't know when it happened, but that girl with her big dreams and that great purse got replaced by a middle-aged woman with a fanny pack. Until I found The 4 Word Answer! Now she and her great accessories are back!*

Welcome home, Elizabeth. Many of us get lost living a life we never chose, never wanted, and never thought would be ours. We are desperate for help with time running out. This is why, over the next six chapters, I will prove to you that *The 4 Word Answer* works—and works fast. It worked for me and countless other people, and it will work for you, too, because what you are about to discover is a story that will change your life forever, a story whose hero isn't Elizabeth or me. It is *you!*

The 4 Word Answer is no fairytale. It is very real. The events and details in this book all happened. The social media posts, emails, and conversations are all raw and honest. No name or incident has been changed. And I cannot wait to share this true, carefully fact-checked, and thoroughly reported book. *The 4 Word Answer* has already transformed my life and the lives of so many others around the world. Now it will do the same for you.

The 4 Word Answer is simple to learn, and once mastered, it will never let you down. When applied, it will change every aspect of your life—love, work, friendships, marriage, dating, weight, money, sex, and, ultimately, you! In fact, once you see what *The 4 Word Answer* does, you won't know how you lived without it; however, it will only work if you believe in the power of words—or, to be precise, the power of four words! This is exactly what happened to Paul:

> *Rob! I was always calling myself and everyone else such horrible things. My marriage and friendships were dead, and I was about to lose my job because of the way I spoke to people. Until I replaced the four-letter word with The 4 Word Answer. I now understand that words are powerful, which is why tonight, I'm telling my wife that I love her. How's that for a four-letter word?*

Paul is not alone. But it's not just words that are powerful. Equally important is how we think and behave and the choices we make. How many times have you wished: If only I were just a little prettier, a little thinner, a little younger, a little smarter, or a little kinder? We have all wondered what life would be like if we had more money or just a little good old-fashioned luck. Who hasn't thought about what would have happened if they had met and fallen in love with someone else? Who hasn't imagined how life would have looked if we had grabbed that one dream that got away? The road of life has many different paths, which is why we all need a little help. Think about how different your journeys would be if you had some assistance guiding you along the way. That is exactly what *The 4 Word Answer* is. It is a map, a compass, to show you the way, to point you toward the road of success and happiness that is right for you.

Do you ever feel stuck in the pages of the story of your life, playing a person you don't want to be? You are not alone. Too many of us are playing a supporting character in our lives. Some of us aren't even playing people we like! No one grew up wanting to be a James Bond villain or an ugly sister in Cinderella! Yet that is exactly who we have become. Ann grew up dreaming of becoming a nurse, of spending her days helping people with expertise and kindness. But instead, she ended up spending every minute of her day with someone she wouldn't want to be friends with—herself.

> Hi Rob — My story got bogged down repeating the same cruel chapter over and over until I found The 4 Word Answer. You taught me that I was the writer of my own story. So that mean character I was playing got written out of the show and was replaced by Ann, the kind nurse I always knew I would be! Thank you.

Think about all the time you have wasted, like Ann, playing the wrong part in life, taking the path that wasn't meant for you. It is so easy to get stuck and trapped and, eventually, give in to who you have become. It doesn't take long before the existence that we didn't choose becomes the reality that we never rejected.

Dreams don't vanish overnight, but they do say goodbye surprisingly fast! Some dreams put up a better fight than others before they are replaced with the same mundane daily routines. No wonder so many people fantasize about starting fresh every New Year's Eve when the clock strikes midnight. Imagine having that opportunity to start over every month, every week, every day, every hour, every second, every moment—in fact, whenever you want. Well, imagine no more because that is exactly what *The 4 Word Answer* teaches you to do. As Tim testifies:

> *I wasted so much time waiting for the perfect moment to change, which never came along. Now I don't waste another minute thanks to The 4 Word Answer. Right now is the right moment to reset your life. I do it every day, several times a day! And that is why I just quit my job after getting into drama school. I have always dreamed of being an actor, and now it's coming true.*

Tim, we can't wait to see you win an Oscar! So, are you ready to restart a new life full of excitement and hope like Tim? Good, because we have all wasted too much time not being the star in our own story. Get ready to be the hero you were always meant to be. Shake off the myth that it is too late or too impossible to change because that is not true. In fact, with *The 4 Word Answer,* it will be impossible *not* to change!

To say that I created *The 4 Word Answer* isn't exactly accurate. What is true is that *The 4 Word Answer* created me. It saved me from the lowest point of my life. As I mentioned, I doubted any of this would work at first. In fact, I didn't believe anything could change my miserable life. Ironically, to the outside world, things couldn't have looked better. I had opened my own public relations company after years of working for someone I didn't like.

I represented some of the biggest stars and brands in the world: Jennifer Lopez, Diddy, Bon Jovi, Alicia Keys, Naomi Campbell, Iyanla Vanzant, *Esquire Magazine*, Kate Spade, MAC Cosmetics, Estée Lauder Companies, British royalty, and even the cat from *Sabrina, the Teenage Witch* (meow)! My working-class family name had no business being above a Tiffany Blue door to an office in Manhattan, yet there it was! It was a door that opened up to Jessica Simpson and her sister Ashlee, Paula Abdul, and even TV's bossy *Bridezillas* clients.

With designer furniture and freshly painted walls, my office on West 26th looked like the American Dream. My personal life and marriage had friends seeing green with envy. And my smile couldn't have glowed any brighter, thanks to Jennifer Hudson's extraordinary dentist, Dr. Debra Glassman, who tended to my mouth free of charge! But what no one could see was that inside, everything was falling apart. Everything about me and my life was a big fat lie. I was a phony, a fake, a fraud! Pretending to be someone else while the real me died a little more each day. My marriage, my career, my finances, and, most importantly, my sense of self couldn't have been any lower—something that Rachel knows all about.

Hello Rob, I'm Rachel. I've got a five-bedroom house in an amazing community. My car still has that new smell, my children go to the best schools, I am a respected member of our community, and my hot husband is hung! I am also up to my eyeballs in debt, my kids hate me, and the big boy is having an affair.

I can't pretend to be someone else anymore. HELP!

You will be happy to know that Rachel is now living in a cute two-bedroom apartment in the city, she's met a new loyal man (we don't know his size!), and she's mending her relationship with her children. The point is, it just goes to prove that not even Dr. Glassman has any idea what is going on behind someone else's closed Tiffany Blue door. Just like Rachel, I was drowning inside while pretending everything was great on the outside! I was living in constant fear of being exposed and couldn't see any way out. Making matters worse, I turned to booze and pills to escape from my life.

Then, one random morning, after crawling out of bed hungover with my head pounding—having no idea how I got home the night before—the solution appeared. Scrolling through unanswered emails with one eye shut and the other barely open, I heard the beginning of what would go on to change my life and the lives of so many others. The beginning of what would become *The 4 Word Answer*.

The answer was literally in the same room with me, scream-ing out to be noticed. At first, it started as only *three* words. Three powerful words that rang through my foggy mind, clear as a bell. They pierced through everything that was going on, to the point where I couldn't shut them up. At that point in my life, it wasn't unusual for me to start my day midmorning, hungover, crying in the bathroom mirror. But that day, I was ready for a change. The tears were different. These were no longer tears of despair; these were tears of joy.

I was unaware at the time that I had found the answer to questions I had never felt smart enough, kind enough, or even important enough to ask. For the first time in my life, I had found a real solution. And this answer changed everything—my career, my marriage, my finances, my happiness, my confidence, and my self-esteem—because it started with me. But I wasn't alone: it happened to Zoe, too.

I found you, Rob, and The 4 Word Answer by chance. Your late-night talk show came on after a show I was watching. It is amazing that you came into my life when I needed the help the most. I couldn't have been lower. I couldn't have needed a friend more. That was when you appeared, completely by accident, with the right words, my four words! Words that changed my life forever.

As you would say, CHEERS!

Cheers to you too, Zoe! But let me be clear: since I started using *The 4 Word Answer* over eight years ago, I haven't transformed into the "perfect" person. Far from it. I could still do with losing ten pounds and not get so bitchy when my handsome husband, Bruce, leaves dirty dishes in the sink. But, like Elizabeth, Paul, Ann, Tim, Rachel, and Zoe, what has changed is that I have discovered the real me. I have found the person I was always meant to be. The person who had been hiding so deep inside for so long that I forgot they ever existed. I found the best possible version of myself and began living my most authentic life. Trust me, I know that person is hiding inside you, too, and together, we will find them.

I have gone from a place where I was constantly worrying about paying my bills on time to having a savings account with over two years' salary in it. I have transformed from being a person who had lost their voice to being called the number one entertainment columnist in America, from being someone who couldn't get out of bed in the morning to being invited to appear on America's number one morning show, *The Today Show*. I regularly spill the tea with the brilliant Wendy Williams on *The Wendy Williams Show*, and I'm booked so often on CNN that hunky Chris Cuomo knows my name. When *Good Day New York* needs a fill-in host, they send a car and driver to take *me* to the studio on 67th street. And when *VH1* wanted to create their own daily live morning show, *The Gossip Table,* they called me. I still can't believe that my many appearances on America's biggest top-forty radio show, *The Elvis Duran Show,* led to me getting my iHeartRadio podcast, *Naughty But Nice with Rob*, which breaks Apple's top-twenty charts on a daily basis, with millions of listeners. Selling out the 92nd Street Y was unforgettable, but playing myself on *Days of Our Lives* was surreal—was I the town of Salem's first English accent?

On a personal level, my relationships are more solid than they have ever been, and my marriage to handsome Bruce has never been stronger, despite our ongoing dishwashing disputes! (Wink.) The pills are gone, and the occasional drink now celebrates life rather than numbs it. In fact, my life has never been better. And it's all because of *The 4 Word Answer*, which is why I have to share it with you.

> *Dear Rob — What a fool I have been for years, being angry and jealous at everyone else's success. The 4 Word Answer has taught me that there is enough for everyone. Sharing doesn't make you smaller, it makes you bigger. I started my own blog, thanks to you, and last week, I got a call from a big TV producer who wants to meet with me about turning it into a TV show! #4WordAnswer —Donny*

I know we are going to be hearing more from Donny, who is right. It is a gift to share, and something as powerful as *The 4 Word Answer* must be spread around like manure (yes, just like manure!) to make all our dreams grow, whatever they may be.

Discover that you decide if you want to be Jack or Jill. The decision to go up that hill or go get a cup of coffee instead is up to you. You have the power to change the ending to the Romeo or Juliet story in your life. If you want them to run off into the sunset and live happily ever after, then that is what will happen. Humpty Dumpty never needs to fall off a wall again if you don't want him to because *your* life is *your* story. Remember, the only person stopping you from being the author of your own life, from writing your own beginning, middle, and ending, is you. Never give that power away to anyone else again. The days of having to grin and bear it are over. It will be impossible for you to "keep calm and carry on" because the knight on a horse coming to save you has arrived, and it is *you*. And as Mary discovered, every great story starts with just a few words—or to be more precise, the right four words!

Dear Rob, I didn't know how to start a new chapter until you gave me the four right words. We only have one life to live, so make sure it is the life you want. Since I started using The 4 Word Answer every day, I have lost 40 lbs. The real Mary is back, thanks to you and four little words.

But don't just take Mary's word for it! Over the next six chapters, I'm going to show you the receipts, as my pal, Wendy Williams, would say. The evidence. The proof that this really works. You are going to see real-life example after example of how many lives have changed, because *The 4 Word Answer* is no longer just my story to tell. It belongs to everyone and anyone who has said the four words. And so, I want to thank all my co-authors, a few of whom you have already met, who helped me write this book.

- Elizabeth, who you might see cavorting around town, swinging her great purse.
- Paul and his lovely wife, who replaced the four-letter word with *The 4 Word Answer*.
- Ann, our favorite nurse, who is not only kind to her patients but also kind to herself.
- Tim, who isn't wasting another minute chasing someone else's dreams.
- Rachel, who is no longer living a lie, worried about impressing others and ignoring herself.
- Zoe, who now has so many friends she doesn't have time to watch TV.

- Donny, who's now so busy on TV that he has hired a team of four with whom he is sharing his success.
- Mary, who starts every morning with four simple words rather than her bathroom scale.

Without these co-authors, and many more I will introduce to you, this book wouldn't exist. And I cannot wait to add your name to this list, too.

Over the next few chapters, we are going to detail every single aspect of who, what, when, where, why, and how *The 4 Word Answer* will work for you. Get ready to unlock the door to happiness and success and slam shut the window on jealousy, worry, and anxiety. And to paraphrase Julie Andrews in *The Sound of Music*, the beginning is always a very good place to start. And if it's good enough for Miss Andrews…!

It was a snowy December night, eight years ago. I was in my office, the one with a Tiffany Blue front door, on 26th Street in New York City. I had just hung up the phone with the editor in chief of *Us Weekly*. I didn't know it at the time, but that's when *The 4 Word Answer* began….

12

2

C
H
A
P
T
E
R

Who Are You In Four Words?

I'M NOT SURE EXACTLY WHEN IT HAPPENED BUT, WITHOUT A doubt, celebrity had become the new religion dominating every aspect of life. The cult of celebrity allowed us to worship at the altar twenty-four seven—which was very good news for me because my entire life revolved around these "gods." If this new "religion" had found a pope in the form of the editor-in-chief of *Us Weekly* or Kim Kardashian, then that made me a cardinal wearing one of the original red power hats who got them elected.

Working for the biggest stars in the world (Jennifer Lopez, P. Diddy, Alicia Keys, and Jessica Simpson) officially as a publicist (but in reality, as a confidant), I had seen it all. During my fifteen years as a celebrity publicist, which even included doing PR for the odd celebrity pooch—Paris Hilton once left her chihuahua in my office and suggested I FedEx "Tinkerbelle" back to LA

—I had wiped away more than my fair share of mascara from the eyes of both famous ladies and men. I had a front-row seat as pop culture history was created, and it bathed me in celebrity tears of pain and joy.

Before Jessica Simpson told then-husband Nick Lachey that they were getting divorced, I remember her calling me. Jon Bon Jovi flew me to his live shows on a private jet to escort out the press before his fabulous hair flopped—a luxury that didn't extend to Richie Sambora! I was responsible for making sure an Asian pear was within feet of Jennifer Lopez at any given moment, per her very specific demands. I was having lunch with Alicia Keys when a reporter asked if she was a lesbian and counseled the then-closeted weatherman, Sam Champion, after a cheeky food writer at *Time Out* announced Mr. Sunshine enjoyed a big piece of meat!

I became that guy, the go-to English chap for celebrity crisis management, with almost every famous train wreck stopping in my station. If you were caught lip-syncing on national TV, don't worry, I'll handle it, Miss Ashlee Simpson. If you lost one of your colored contact lenses that turned your dark eyes blue, I was your guy, Miss Hilton. Even if you were accused of assaulting your housekeeper, Miss Campbell would call me. Hell, once I was even spotted taking a fresh linen napkin to carefully pat dry the sweet Cîroc sweat off Diddy's brow! Simply put, I had perfected the job of being invisible while making everyone else shine. Like Houdini, I could disappear, making me literally one of the queens behind the scenes!

The *New York Observer* boldly announced, "In the basement boiler room of the celebrity-industrial complex, burned by its machinery but still pulling the levers, is a man named Rob Shuter." Kate Spade called me Mary Poppins, which was much more pleasant than being called a burn victim! To quote dear Katy, may she rest in peace, I was "practically perfect in every way." And just like everyone's favorite nanny, I was able to handle any predicament with a spoonful of sugar!

However, all this didn't start out looking quite so supercalifragilisticexpialidocious. I was an annoyingly happy twenty-year-old when I moved to America for a summer to be with my new American boyfriend. We had met while I was selling ice cream at the Playhouse Theatre in Edinburgh, Scotland. Bruce, the super talented new boyfriend, had turned his Grammy award-winning hit song, "Copacabana," which he wrote with Barry Manilow—yes, that "Copacabana," with Lola, a yellow feather, and that dress cut down to there!—into a musical that was trying out in Scotland before it went on to its smash-hit West End debut. I was up North for a slightly less glamorous reason: I was studying at the University of Edinburgh to get my master's degree in political science. But just like my talented new guy, I was also trying out, hoping to do so well that I, too, could head down to the capital with my degree in hand, a dream in my heart, and make an equally thrilling London debut. (Note: Bruce and I are still together, and even married, thanks to *The 4 Word Answer*. And yes, Barry Manilow does give the best wedding gifts!) And while Bruce's glorious West End debut went ahead as scheduled, my plans changed. My master's degree and I were no longer heading to London. Instead, we were heading to New York City!

With a lot of help from Bruce and his fancy friends, I got a job interning at Boneau/Bryan Brown, the world's leading theatrical press agency. I was hooked on show business right away. Studying the great political thinkers in Scotland, Hegel, Marx, and Nietzsche, couldn't compete with Liza Minnelli and Third Fork From The Right in Broadway's *Beauty and the Beast*! After graduating (with that master's, did I mention that?), I moved to America full-time to be with the man who really did write the songs that made the whole world sing. And I quickly progressed from being a star-struck Broadway intern to landing my first real-life, high-powered adult job. I became a receptionist!

Answering phones, getting coffee, and filing papers at the newly opened New York offices of Los Angeles-based publicity power firm Bragman Nyman Cafarelli was the opportunity of a lifetime. Being LA-based, Bragman Nyman Cafarelli had little interest in legit theatre. No, this company represented "real" stars: A-lister clients like Cameron Diaz, Kate Hudson, Vanessa Williams, Whoopi Goldberg, and Barry Manilow (now you know how I got the job!). This meant my days of singing silverware were long behind me. Every time I answered the phone and sang, "Bragman Nyman Cafarelli. This is Rob Shuter," I would get a thrill! From where I started in life, in a down-on-its-luck former industrial town in the Midlands of England, I was the first member of my family to make it to university and already felt like a winner. I would never have dared to dream big enough to land a position at a company like this!

In the beginning, I would sit around doing nothing while waiting for the phones to ring, practicing saying the rather tricky "Bragman Nyman Cafarelli" over and over again in my inner voice so no one would detect that I had a slight lisp. Surprisingly, it turned out that not as many people as you think wanted to talk about Ms. Goldberg or Ms. Diaz on any given day. Most people assume the answer will be no, so they never ask! Thus, I would sit and wait for any sign of life from the outside world as I sorted through the office mail. That's when I discovered magazines. (Note to our younger readers: magazines are pages of words that are too interesting for the internet yet not interesting enough to be in a book!) I devoured every single one from cover to cover. It was a time when the great Kevin Sessums and witty George Wayne were still writing for *Vanity Fair* and long before Anna Wintour at *Vogue* knew what a Justin Bieber was!

When the phones did ring, interrupting my educational reading, it was usually one of the agency's clients calling themselves. As I found myself spending more and more time talking with all these extraordinary creatures (because even when you are paying $8,000 a month, it doesn't guarantee your publicist will take your calls), I became more and more comfortable around them. At first, they usually just wanted reservations to places I had never been. But thanks to my new literature, I knew about it all! If you wanted to pretend to be cultured but couldn't get through an opera, I would recommend *Phantom*! And if you wanted to be spotted, the best photo-op in town is still Nobu!

It wasn't long before I started escorting clients through the rounds of TV shows based in New York. As we traveled together in their fancy chauffeur-driven cars, we would play the question-and-answer game: we would practice answering the questions I knew Robin Roberts or someone you have never heard of at E! was about to ask and try to work out a clever way to plug whatever they were promoting in every answer! "Thank you, Robin. What do I think about racism in Hollywood? My movie comes out this Friday!" As well as the clients, I got to know the celebrity reporters, photographers, producers, and bookers at the outlets in the Big Apple's fruit bowl. I even became friendly with the most feared gossip columnists in town. They ran the pages that celebrities with talent tried to keep out of and celebrities with none begged to get into—yes, I'm talking about you, Bethenny Frankel!

As much as I enjoyed my new powerful media contacts, it was my relationships with clients that I loved. Fame is intoxicating, and by spending time with my increasingly large army of D-listers as we worked together in their homes, cars, trips, and on many, many ledges, I made a name for myself as someone who would not only always take their calls but also work hard to understand who they were. It was like being best friends with the most popular kids in school and hanging with the cool kids who normally wouldn't want anything to do with me! Although it never happens overnight, the truth is that is exactly how it felt. One day I woke up, and my D-listers had become C-listers. Then seemingly just as fast, my C-listers transformed into B-listers. All it would take was for one of them to land an A-list project, like when Kelly Ripa left *All My Children* to sit next to Regis, and my career would change forever, along with theirs. I waited patiently until, one day, my phone rang with an opportunity that was even better than an A-list star. It was from an A-list institution.

Like Kelly, I had found my Regis when I was offered a position at Dan Klores Communications, one of the most respected publicity power players in the business and the place that anyone who was anyone called when in trouble. They were the crisis managers to everyone who was anyone, from heiress Paris Hilton, socialite Lizzie Grubman, supermodel Naomi Campbell, and P. Diddy—who needs no introduction. They all solicited the help of DKC in times of need—on the heels of a sex tape, a hit and run, abusing a maid, and gunshots—all alleged! It was at DKC that my career hit a different celebrity stratosphere: Jennifer Lopez, Jessica Simpson, Alicia Keyes, Bon Jovi, Kate Spade, Kimora Lee Simmons, and even Her Royal Highness Princess Michael of Kent—the original "Princess Pushy"—all became my clients.

These avatars of human beings were inspiring, and I was eager to soak up all their secrets to success. Joan Rivers explained to me that there were a lot of people funnier than she was, but she would stand in the rain longer than any of them. When most went home soaking wet, Joan was still standing. But at this level of the game, drive and talent were not enough. No, the only thing all these people had in common is that they *knew exactly who they are.*

Every super-successful person I have ever met could describe themselves in just a few simple words! It was the most important question a personality or brand would answer: "Who are you?" Only those comfortable enough in their own skin knew the answer. And only those who knew the answer would be successful. The best could tell you in just four words! Hours and hours are spent every day around the world trying to get to the essence of each celebrity and brand. Entire marketing, branding, and PR departments' only job is to figure this out and then promote it. And this is why I found myself writing down on yellow Post-its the four words that described each and every one of my clients. The notes were attached to my computer screen so I could never forget them. One word per Post-it. Four Post-its per client. Boom! There it was, looking right at me, reminding and guiding every decision like a celebrity North Star! Every opportunity that came across my desk had to fit at least three of the four words to get a yes. Anything less would be guaranteed a no.

At first, I got off to a bit of a rocky start, which always happens when you jump in uninformed. Diddy had aggressively rejected a press release I'd whipped up announcing another one of his famous White Parties. It was beautifully written, contained all the right information, correct grammar, and spelling that would make any English teacher proud. But what it didn't contain was the correct amount of Diddy-ness. I had foolishly ignored the four-word rule!

"I would never say that!" Puffy snapped at me, reading the release. "This isn't who I am! This isn't my brand!" He was right. I returned to my desk to try again. Determined not to make the same mistake, I recited the four words that told me who Diddy was over and over before giving it another shot. "Diddy Puts The Man Back Into Manhattan Party" came pouring out. Of course, he loved it!

It wasn't long before I knew everything about each of my clients: what they would say, what they would wear, what they would do, and what they would think. I had the answers to questions before they were asked. It almost felt like cheating, getting a sneak peek at the picture to a massive jigsaw puzzle before being handed a thousand pieces. Knowing their strengths and weaknesses, likes and dislikes, beliefs and values, and what they were good at and what they were bad at made it much easier to succeed.

Sometimes I would catch myself thinking, "How did this working-class lad from the Midlands, who didn't know his Dolce from his Gabbana, end up on a private yacht in Cannes owned by the Cipriani family?" I was a seabound Cinderella, watching beautiful Naomi Campbell open up birthday gifts that had been messengered over by water taxi from, you guessed it, Dolce and Gabbana themselves! But before I could answer that question, it all fell apart. I was fired! The yacht turned back into a pumpkin, the seahorses back into mice, and the beautiful people into ugly sisters who stopped returning my calls. It was over as quickly as it had started, and all I was left with was a bunch of yellow Post-its!

Desperation kicks in fast when you have no money coming in and a lot of expenses going out. After just a few months, I had gotten to the point where I could barely pay off my ever-increasing minimum payments due. All the while, I was praying for a miracle to come along and save me—which, of course, it never did and never does. Yet, as bad as things were with my finances, money wasn't my primary concern. Shame won that prize! I spent hours worrying about the humiliation, concerned about what people would think. Disgrace, discomfort, and indignity filled my mind. At first, I pretended I had quit. I told everyone I chose to leave my fabulous A-list clients behind because I was working on something new and exciting, a project that I couldn't say too much about…because it didn't exist. People I had known for years, folks I once called friends, moved on faster than an Olsen sister at an all-you-can-eat buffet. I had more contacts in my phone than Siri, but few of them called. I wanted to rise like a phoenix for all the wrong reasons. I wanted to shout from the skyscrapers of Manhattan, "Rob Shuter is still successful." But instead, I sat alone in silence.

I had gone from popping out of bed each morning like a piece of toast to dreading the long day that lay ahead. Some mornings, I couldn't get up at all, and at night, it was impossible to sleep. Lying awake with all my problems rattling around my head, feeling worthless and humiliated had become my new routine. Misery was now my full-time job! As the days turned into weeks and months, my problems got worse. That's when I reached for help!

Not the kind of help that works, mind you. No, instead, I grabbed for the kind of help that was guaranteed to make things worse. I turned to booze and pills to dull my feelings of failure. Feeling numb sure beat feeling defeated. I was drowning, and the more I struggled to pretend everything was swimming along just fine, the deeper I sank. Some days were so bad I couldn't get out of bed at all. The days I did get up, I couldn't recognize the person looking back at me in the mirror. Bloated from the alcohol and pills, both of which had become my major daily food groups, the guy in my bathroom was unrecognizable. I was forty something years old and without a job. But it was more than that. I hadn't just lost my job. I had lost my identity. I had lost myself!

For the last decade, I had been the Mary Poppins of PR— Kate Spade had told me so herself! My job had been my alma mater, where I was the star pupil. But Jessica Simpson's publicist is not Jessica Simpson, in the same way that a garden tool is not the beautiful garden. My entire identity had belonged to someone else. At best, I was a spoke in the wheel of their success—which explains why I could be fired with such ease while their lives rolled on unchanged without me. Yet, when they left my life, the wheels fell off. Without them, I couldn't move!

The truth was I didn't want to go back to pretending to be someone else. I also didn't want to be the person I was right then. I wanted to move forward and be the real me. I wanted to be someone who fixed their broken life and soul. I didn't want to play the villain in my own story or the hero in someone else's! It was time for me to find a new story, to say goodbye to my Houdini past and hello to a new narrative where the hero was me, lisp and all. I needed to be annoyingly happy again and feel like a winner with my degree in my hand and a dream back in my heart! Did I mention I had a master's degree? I could no longer wait for a Regis. I needed to save myself! The problem was I didn't know how!

My life had become so dazed and confused that it often felt like a blur; however, I will never forget what happened on that rainy morning. It was July 16th, my birthday. I was standing in my bathroom, crying as the TV played an old movie in the background. That was when I heard the words that would change my life forever! "You is **kind**. You is **smart**. You is **important**," said the maid to a little girl in the film. I froze as the words kept playing over and over in my head. **Kind. Smart. Important.** The words felt familiar and not just because I had seen the film before. I knew those words. I hadn't heard them in a long time, but I felt like I was reconnecting with an old friend. A cool friend I used to hang out with all the time. I not only heard them, but I could see them. Written out on yellow Post-its in my mind. It was like seeing a face from the past that you couldn't quite place right away, someone you had once been well acquainted with who now felt like a stranger. "You is **kind**. You is **smart**. You is **important**." These words had surrounded me for years, but they hadn't belonged to me. Then it clicked. I knew exactly who they belonged to.

Racing out of the bathroom, I pulled out the boxes that were hiding beneath my bed. They had arrived from my office the day after I was fired, but it had been too painful to open them since they'd shown up so rudely unannounced. That morning, it was different. I was a man on a mission. I was searching for a clue to point me in the right direction. Yet, all I found was a bunch of old files, schedules, and press releases from a former life. Digging deeper, though, I discovered an envelope full of the Post-its, each containing just one word. There must have been a hundred of them. I started to read them out loud, one at a time. After a few dozen or so, I froze. All these words on the Post-its had something in common that I had never seen before. A pattern started to emerge. These seemingly random words were not random at all. They were connected, falling into clear categories—**kind**, **smart**, and **important**.

This was the secret to success! Every single famous person I knew was **kind** enough to themselves to be comfortable in their own skin. They were all **smart** enough to believe in their authentic self. And every single one of them believed they were **important** enough to step out from even the largest shadow. I knew in that moment that this was going to be the key to my success too. "You is **kind**. You is **smart**. You is **important**," I said to myself out loud as I wrote the words down. One word per Post-it. Three, and eventually, four Post-its per Rob—we will get to that in chapter 6! There it was, looking right at me, my own North Star guiding me to success! Now, every opportunity that came across into my life had to fit at least three of the four words to get a yes. Anything less would be guaranteed a no. I headed to the kitchen, knowing who I was, to find my phone, no longer assuming the answer would be no. The annoyingly happy me was back, and this time, I wasn't going to let him go away again! I had found the answer. Or rather, the answer found me.

It will work for you, too. No master's degree or spoonful of sugar required. That was how *The 4 Word Answer* was born.

3

You Is Kind!

KINDNESS IS ESSENTIAL TO FINDING SUCCESS AND HAPPINESS. Maybe even more surprising, it is the one of the four words that describes every single person who has found both.

"When you've worked hard, and done well, and walked through that doorway of opportunity, you do not slam it shut behind you. You reach back and you give other folks the same chances that helped you succeed," said Michelle Obama, beautifully describing most people's definition of pure **kindness**. A **kindness** that focuses on helping others, reaching out to a friend or even a stranger in times of need and expecting nothing in return. Think about the last time someone was **kind** to you. Didn't it feel great? Now, think about the last time you did something **kind** for someone else—felt even better, didn't it? This only adds to the mystery of why we are not **kind** more often! However, there is another

form of **kindness** that is even rarer than what the former First Lady describes, a **kindness** that not only makes you feel great, but also makes your chances of success greater, too—it is being **kind** to yourself!

Kindness isn't the first thing that comes to mind when you think about celebrities, yet I promise you it is central to their success. I have seen firsthand that no one is **kinder** to themselves than Jennifer Lopez, Jessica Simpson, Alicia Keys, and Diddy. They have all mastered this revolutionary form of **kindness**, graduating with flying colors from the university of being **kind** to themselves. Let me be clear! I'm not saying you shouldn't be grateful when someone holds open the door of success for you or disappointed when someone slams it shut after they have walked through it themselves. No, what I am saying is you need to be **kind** enough to yourself to open the door to opportunity on your own. You need to have the confidence to push it wide open with whatever it takes before you strut through like a peacock! People who are **kind** to themselves know their worth. When you start thinking, learning, understanding, and practicing this special form of **kindness**, you will be a star in your own life!

We all have been taught to only think about **kindness** in the Michelle Obama way. While I am in no way discouraging being **kind** to others, I am encouraging—in fact, I'm insisting—that we all start being **kind** to ourselves first. Princess Diana said, *"Carry out a random act of* **kindness***, with no expectation of reward, safe in the knowledge that one day someone might do the same for you."* But, with all due respect, this is only half the story. Where might you be right now if your parents, friends, teachers, and idols had all encouraged you to be **kinder** to yourself?

THE 4 WORD ANSWER

Putting ourselves first isn't something that a lot of us practice, but those who do thrive.

Some will argue that this revolutionary version of **kindness** is selfish. But they are wrong. To quote RuPaul, *"If you don't love yourself, how in the hell you gonna love somebody else?"* The same is true with **kindness**. If you aren't **kind** to yourself, how in the hell are you going to be **kind** to someone else? The time has come for this new definition of **kindness** to no longer be just for the few rich, famous, and successful people. We all need to remove any purity test and questions about motivations surrounding being **kind**. Instead, join the rule breakers and mavericks, such as Lady Gaga, who have all embraced the fact that the greatest act of **kindness** we can ever give is to ourselves.

> *"I've been searching for ways to heal myself, and I've found that **kindness** is the best way."*
> —Lady Gaga

After years of watching and working with extraordinary people, it became clear that it doesn't matter why you are **kind** to yourself or others—the end result will be the same. I remember volunteering at Gay Men's Health Crisis in New York City before I got my work permit. The staffer in charge said something that sounded so strange at the time but now makes total sense. He said, "I don't care why you are here today. You can be volunteering because you want to help others. Or you can be volunteering because you want to meet cute guys. Maybe you are here just trying to show your friends that you are a good person, or you want to show yourself that you are a good person…. It doesn't matter, because ultimately it will all lead to the same result." Amen, he is right! As philosopher Eric Hoffer puts it, *"**Kindness** can become* *its own motive. We are made **kind** by being **kind**."* Stop thinking about the why and start thinking about the when and to whom you are going to be **kind** (hint: like right now to yourself)!

Nothing Is Kinder Than Accepting Yourself

Acceptance is the cornerstone of **kindness**, which is why you must accept yourself. This doesn't happen in an hour, a day, or a week, but rather, to be totally comfortable in your own skin is a lifelong struggle that needs constant attention. The more you practice, the easier it becomes, yet it is always something requiring constant focus and attention. That is why you need to think about it every single day until it becomes a habit, a way of life as natural as breathing and waking up in the morning, and even then, don't lose your focus!

> *"My happiness grows in direct proportion to my acceptance, and in inverse proportion to my expectations."*
> —Michael J. Fox

Most people think acceptance is being totally honest with yourself about everything that you are; however, it is also about being totally honest and comfortable with everything you are not. Envy and jealousy are helpful indicators that you have not yet fully accepted yourself. Desiring what other people have means you still have work to do! It is only when you truly accept your own success, beauty, and talent that you can be 100 percent at peace with yourself. And this is only possible once you stop beating yourself up and embrace where you are and where you are not in your life right now!

"Your imperfections make you beautiful, they make you who you are. So just be yourself, love yourself for who you are and just keep going."
—Demi Lovato

Stop racing through life toward the finish line and start enjoying the journey along the way. It is very easy to take life for granted. One example is rushing from appointment to appointment and missing all the wonderful small moments that happen in between. When you only think about checking off each task on your to-do list and moving on to the next, you fall into the trap of finding more and more stuff, rather than finding true happiness. This is how I went about each day of my life for years until a former client and friend of mine committed suicide. I will never forget the moment I found out that dear Kate Spade had passed. I was running to a TV interview, frustrated that I couldn't find a taxi. But finding out about her death, I realized that no matter how famous, rich, or successful you are, we all eventually reach the same real finish line: death. An end no one should be rushing to get to! So slow down, do not speed up. And always be **kind** enough to yourself to accept and live in the moment.

"The acceptance of death gives you more of a stake in life, in living life happily, as it should be lived. Living for the moment."
—Sting

> *I would beat myself up over the feeling that I wasn't moving fast enough in life to accomplish everything I wanted to get done. But in the end, the only thing I achieved was complete burnout. Then I found The 4 Word Answer, and everything changed. It has taught me to slow down and smell the roses! Now, the only thing I wish I had done quicker is accept myself, which takes* **kindness**, *not speed! Thanks.* —Rebecca

Like Rebecca, there was a point in my life when I would beat myself up, too. I couldn't remember a time when I didn't think about my big nose, my soft jawline that made it difficult to know where my neck began, and my bad skin! My arm that had been so damaged at birth that I came very close to having it amputated didn't help me feel like a movie star! For years, I longed to be super handsome with two perfect arms. I dreamed about how different my life would be if I had skin like Brad Pitt! It wasn't just my physical appearance that I was so unkind about. I was equally cruel about feeling like I was "not enough." Not an opportunity passed me by that I wouldn't use to feel even worse, comparing myself to those richer, more handsome, more popular, and more perfect than me. Until *The 4 Word Answer* gave me another way at looking at my perceived ugly imperfections!

> *"Perfect is boring. Human is beautiful."*
> —Tyra Banks

Now I choose to stand up against the relentless bully inside my head because, for the first time in my life, I have accepted myself. I know what I am and what I am not, and I have finally made peace with both. Now, instead of being brutal, I am compassionate. Now instead of judging, I embrace acceptance. Now, instead of choosing to be cruel, I choose to be **kind**.

> *"I'm a big believer in accepting yourself and not really worrying about it."*
>
> —Jennifer Lawrence

The Cruelest Thing You Say to Yourself

Paul McCartney (yes, that Paul McCartney, the Beatle) said that even as the world's most successful living songwriter and performer, worth over $1 billion, he still hears a cruel internal voice telling him that he isn't "good enough." If Paul hears it, so does everyone else, including you!

This voice in your head telling you, 'You can't! You won't! You'll never!' is a voice that steals happiness and joy from millions of people around the world every day. Can you imagine how many brilliant songs, novels, plays, cures for diseases, or just happy days we have been robbed of because of this voice? What has it stolen from you? The belief that you are not "good enough" can stop anyone—even the most accomplished among us—from pursuing our dreams, even though it is telling you a lie. It's an echo, repeating the cruel things others have told you before. Things that were not true then and are not true now.

> *"I remind myself to be **kind** to myself, and as slightly ridiculous as it may sound, to treat myself*

*in the same gentle way I'd want to treat a daughter
of mine. It really helps."*

—Emma Stone

Over my years working with some of the most successful
people in the world, I have seen firsthand that they often are
not the most talented. It isn't talent that Jennifer Lopez, Diddy,
Jon Bon Jovi, Alicia Keys, and Jessica Simpson all have in common. No, what they share is the ability to silence the "I'm not
good enough" voice. Sure, like Paul McCartney, there are still
moments of doubt, but it is the way they handle these fears that
free them to succeed—and just like it did for Claire below, it will
work for you, too.

> Before The 4 Word Answer, I was riddled with self-
> doubt and fear. I was constantly scared and fright-
> ened to the point where I was immobilized. I would
> second-guess myself so much that I became invisible.
> I stopped contributing ideas at work and instead spent
> the entire meeting taking notes of other people's com-
> ments. Now, when these voices come creeping back,
> I raise my hand and speak out loud to shut them up.
> Thanks! —Claire

It is almost impossible to completely erase these nasty voices
inside your head, but you can turn down the volume to a whis-
per. The only way to crush the nasty voices is by going after your
dreams, no matter what the voices or anyone else tell you! Taking
action and believing in yourself are the best ways to prove them
all wrong. Stop calling yourself or others names by turning up

the volume of **kindness**. Don't let yourself be defined by the worst moments of your life. Or reduced to the things about you that you hate. The truth is you are "good enough."

> *"I think no matter what you look like, the key is to first of all be happy with yourself. And when you know if you want to try to improve things that you don't like about yourself, then do it after you appreciate yourself."*
>
> —Adele

Think of the most successful people you know personally, your boss or a friend or relative who has done very well for themselves. Realize that they have no more God-given talent than you. In fact, when it comes to natural gifts, most of us have about the same. There are far more "ordinary" people in this world than extraordinarily talented. In fact, it is super rare to find someone who is truly exceptional, brilliant, and dazzling—which is why when we do, we call it extraordinary.

> *"Success is just a war of attrition. Sure, there's an element of talent you should probably possess. But if you just stick around long enough, eventually something is going to happen."*
>
> —Dax Shepard

When you get nervous or frightened about trying something new, think about the most average people you are aware of who have achieved the greatest success. I think of Sarah Palin—the Sarah Palin who ran for vice president of the United States, the second-most powerful person in the free world! I have her autobiography on my desk and every time I think I can't do something or that I'm not good enough, I place my hand on it. Before going on TV, I visualize the adorable face of Bravo's Andy Cohen, the most successful average guy on TV, to calm my nerves. You see, I don't have the comedic talent of Jimmy Fallon or the razor-sharp wit of Stephen Colbert, but I can dish about *The Real Housewives*! The next time you start calling yourself cruel names, or when those nasty negative voices pop up in your head, stop and think about your Sarah and Andy! I promise you they are both much **kinder** to themselves than you are.

> *"Success is not final, failure is not fatal: it is the courage to continue that counts."*
> —Winston Churchill

Today I thought about my very average, but very successful, Uncle Terry and then raised my hand in the meeting. Even though my voice was trembling, I finally found the courage to speak up. I'm not going to sit in silence anymore. And guess what, my boss loved my idea. —Heather

As someone who has made my living out of giving an opinion and not necessarily the best one, I couldn't be prouder of you, Heather. Find your voice and express your point of view. I remember when Jennifer Lopez once asked me what color shoes she should wear, red or black? The color wasn't important but having an answer was. Jennifer was testing me, as neither choice was right or wrong. I said "red," and she agreed, although she would have had the same response if I had said "black." Jen never values someone else's opinion more than she values her own. The only person who has 100 percent of all the information about everything going on in each of our lives is ourselves! Making you the only person who knows what's best for you. People are always going to have something to say about you, and the more successful you become, the more opinions you are going to get! Can you imagine being Ariana Grande reading your social media each day? Or Beyoncé checking out NaughtyGossip.com every night? My point is, you can never get away from opinions, but you can stop them from influencing your life. An opinion is not a fact. Let's say that again: an opinion is not a fact! This is why you must make sure you speak up, listen to what you have to say, and be sure that your opinion comes from a place of **kindness**, knowing you really are "good enough."

> *"Your self-worth is determined by you. You don't have to depend on someone telling you who you are."*
> —Beyoncé

Choose your words carefully because, before too long, you will believe them. They have great power and will define you. Cut out the negative and replace it with words of love, respect, and **kindness**. If you wouldn't say it to someone you care about, why are you saying it to yourself? The most important relationship you will ever have in your entire life is with you, so cherish it and be as **kind** to yourself as you are to others.

Now that we know what we must never say to ourselves, let's learn a word we should all be saying much more: "No." No is a complete sentence. Never forget that you do not need to explain yourself. Jessica Simpson, Alicia Keys, Jennifer Lopez, Diddy, and even Sir Paul McCartney are all very comfortable with it. Know that **kindness** requires saying no a lot. Saying no is the only way of saying yes to happiness and success.

> *"People think focus means saying yes to the thing you've got to focus on. But that's not what it means at all. It means saying no to the hundred other good ideas that there are. You have to pick carefully. I'm actually as proud of the things we haven't done as the things I have done. Innovation is saying no to 1,000 things."*
>
> —Steve Jobs

Do This When People Can't Be Kind to You!

We all deserve to have a squad that cheers us on. A team of supporters that celebrates and encourages our success. The only way to get such a squad is to build it. Surround yourself with people who are **kind** and have your best interests at heart. This starts with you. Recruit yourself first! Get into the habit of cheering yourself and your friends on, because the only reason people cannot be happy for others is that they can't be happy for themselves.

> *"Our true friends are those who are with us when the good things happen. They cheer us on and are pleased by our triumphs. False friends only appear at difficult times, with their sad, supportive faces, when, in fact, our suffering is serving to console them for their miserable lives."*
>
> —Paulo Coelho

When you are **kind** to yourself, you will be the first person to jump to your feet, screaming and whooping when you and your pal succeed, knowing that the way you react to other's people's news says more about you than anyone else's achievements. Remember that the next time someone doesn't give you the response you want, it's their problem, not yours. Tune out all who try to discourage you because you don't need anyone's permission to go after your goals. You show everyone, including yourself, who you are by your actions. Be the person who is happy for others' success and surround yourself with folks who are just as excited for you. Trying to win support from people who cannot be excited for you is a losing game, a game that you can only win when you stop playing.

> *"Love yourself first and everything else falls into line. You really have to love yourself to get anything done in this world."*
>
> —Lucille Ball

That is exactly what Gina did.

Once I became my own cheerleader, I attracted like-minded people who couldn't wait to cheer me on. Now my group of friends and I all support each other, but I won't forget it all started with me supporting myself. The 4 Word Answer wins!

Has your day ever been ruined because of the inconsiderate actions of another person? I know mine has. Recently, I got a nasty message from someone who watched me on *The Today*

Show with Hoda Kotb. They were upset with how my right arm "just hung there" as I dished about the latest ongoing Kardashian drama. This person was surprised that anyone with such a noticeable disability was a regular guest on America's number one morning show! It hurt. The old me would have spiraled down a deep, dark tunnel, ignoring the success of being asked to sit next to Hoda, and instead focusing on that one negative voice in the darkness! I would have let a total stranger ruin my day, my week, and possibly my next few months. But not after *The 4 Word Answer.* Now, I realize the only reason people attack is that they are in pain. They can't show any **kindness** to others because they don't show **kindness** to themselves. The next time someone is cruel to you, remember that the cruel comment is not about you. It is about them trying to tear you down to build themselves up.

> *"Ignore the naysayers. Really, the only option is head down and focus on the job."*
> —Chris Pine

Just like Samantha, we are far too kind to ourselves to fall for that trick!

Hi Rob, I'm Samantha, but I'm thinking of changing my name to Taylor 'Shake it Off' Swift! I used to spend hours overanalyzing what people said to me, while they didn't spend a minute thinking about me. You have taught me how to brush off other's opinions, because the only person with the power to make or break my day is me, Samantha SWIFT!

Start removing anyone from your life who doesn't bring you happiness. Get their negative noise out of your head and stop giving access to your time and attention to people who don't deserve it. Think of your thoughts and feelings as two very precious possessions that need to be fiercely protected. Without any apology, learn to be brutal when it comes to your happiness, including your online and social media life. I call it my "attention diet." I write down the names of every person who has entered my head each day, similar to a more traditional diet where you keep track of everything that enters your mouth! Take a long look at that list and perform little audits, or "attention diet," where you increase the portion size of everyone who brings you happiness and joy and cut out all the bad apples who leave a nasty taste in your mouth—especially those people who are constantly saying "sorry."

> *"I'm sooooooo sorry to Taylor Swift and her fans and her mum. I spoke to her mother right after and she said the same thing my mother would've said. She is very talented! I like the lyrics about being a cheerleader and she's in the bleachers! I'm in the wrong for going on stage and taking away from her moment!"* He continued, *"I'm not crazy y'all, I'm just real. Sorry for that!!! I really feel bad for Taylor and I'm sincerely sorry!!! Much respect!!!"*
> —Kanye West

He also apologized on *The Tonight Show with Jay Leno*—and then did so again a year later.

You know who they are, the people, like Kanye, who keep apologizing and then keep doing the same thing over and over again because they are not really sorry. Rather, what they are doing is trying to make themselves feel better. We don't have time for that! Moving forward, a change in behavior is the only apology that should be accepted, and if they won't change, you have to. If they can't be **kind**, they have to go!

> *"Girls, you've gotta know when it's time to turn the page."*
>
> —Tori Amos

A lesson Lorie knows only too well.

> *Why didn't I use the mute button before? I wasted so much time making excuses for other people's bad behavior and accepting fake apologies from jerks in my life. Thanks to The [4 Word] Answer, I realize that you can't change other people, but you can walk away. Rob, my sneakers are on, and I'm running. The 4 Word [Answer] rules — Lorie xoxoxo.*

But what can you do with people you can't run away from? The mean boss that you can't escape from right now because you need the money, or the family member who just cannot be happy for you, but you still care about them? (You know who I am talking about!) When you can't unfriend or cut them out, the only answer is empathy. Instead of getting hurt, get empathetic. When they can't show **kindness**, you must. This doesn't excuse what they are doing for one second, but it does explain it. The next time a parent disapproves, or a boss doesn't understand, stop and think about their life. I guarantee, the crueler they are, the more pain they are in.

"The opposite of anger is not calmness, it's empathy."
—Dr. Mehmet Oz

No one understands this better than Patty.

> I spent my entire life fighting with my mom until I found The 4 Word Answer! It doesn't stop the pain, but knowing why my mom is jealous of me and my life has helped. Rob, empathy has become my superhero cape! Love, Patty

Patty's mom isn't able to see that her jealousy isn't about her daughter; it is about herself and those dreams that are deep inside her that were never realized. Jealousy is a cry for attention from passions that want to be fulfilled. And so, we must stop thinking about it as a bad thing. Instead, we need to see it as a lighthouse, pointing us toward what will make us happy. Jealous feelings are a powerful map, showing you what you really want in life. Sit up and pay attention because those feelings are teaching you about yourself, not anyone else. Follow them like a compass, and they will show you where you want to be in life. Don't forget that there's enough room for everyone to succeed, including you. Someone else's success doesn't make you a failure because you're not in a competition with anyone besides yourself.

"Resentment is like drinking poison and waiting for the other person to die."
—Carrie Fisher

You Are Not Broken—but This Is!

So many people ask, "What is wrong with me?" Goodness knows how many times I have asked myself the same question! Finally, I have an answer after years of searching. Do you really want to know what is "wrong" with you? Absolutely *nothing*...except the way you have been thinking about yourself.

There were years in my life when not a day went by where I didn't tell myself that I sucked. Every hour, I would ask myself, "What the hell is wrong with you?" I had become infected by a cruel pattern of thinking, a virus that allowed negative thoughts to flood my body and take over my mind. Until *The 4 Word Answer* gave me the much-needed medicine that gave me a brand-new way to think about myself, based on being **kind** to the most important person in my life: me!

> *"We just need to be kinder to ourselves. If we treated ourselves the way we treated our best friend, can you imagine how much better off we would be?"*
> —Meghan Markle

Now, when negative thoughts start to come creeping back in, I cut myself a break and focus on something positive to counterbalance them, flipping the cruel thoughts on their head right away before they take over and become a conversation I cannot win. The second they start, stop them in their tracks before they can take root. There is nothing you are thinking that can't be reversed and seen from a different angle because you are in control of your mind. You have a choice between negative and positive, between cruel and **kind**. Train yourself to always choose the optimistic path, and before you know it, the new, brighter way

42

will become your default setting, where you land when you are in neutral. For example, instead of telling yourself, "I don't know anything," say, "I can't wait to learn all this!" Instead of saying, "Everyone hates me," start thinking, "I love myself, and I'm excited to meet people who get me, too." Instead of snapping, "I'm ugly," focus on what you love about yourself—those gorgeous eyes, bright smile, thick hair, or cute feet!

> *"I say if I'm beautiful. I say if I'm strong. You will not determine my story—I will."*
>
> —Amy Schumer

It worked for Kim and Jane:

> *I had a breakthrough today. Instead of calling myself fat, I said I'm pretty and I have got the discipline and focus to lose 10lbs. I signed up for two classes at my local gym. XOXO KIM!*

> *I put The 4 Word Answer in motion today. I was kind to myself and stopped the name-calling after 35 years! I cut those cruel thoughts off the minute they tried to sneak back into my head. I got this! And I'm going to talk with my boss this afternoon about my goals, because I am worth it! Thank you. I am optimistic about what he's going to say, and if he says no, I'm going to try again in 6 months. —Jane*

Good for you, Jane! You believe in yourself and know that optimism is not about believing the answer will always be yes; it's about choosing to believe that when you do get a no, you can handle it. Don't give up! You are much stronger than you think and have already overcome so much in your life. Just think about all the moments when you felt broken, when you were not sure that you would go on. Somehow you got back up and lived another day. The truth is, the only thing in life that can break us is the broken way we think about ourselves.

> *"Smile and let everyone know that today, you're a lot stronger than you were yesterday."*
> —Drake

I wasted way too much time focusing on my right arm when I was younger, thinking I was damaged and flawed. Hiding whenever someone pulled out a camera and disappearing rather than having to shake hands! In reality, the only thing that was wrong with me was the way I thought about myself. I spent years trying to conceal that I am gay. Bumping into friends from school, heading into the big city on a Saturday night on the same number fifty-one bus, I feared I wouldn't be able to explain where I was going and would have my dirty little secret exposed, outing me to the people I loved. I wasn't doing anything wrong or breaking any laws; it was the way I thought about myself that was wrong and should have been illegal because there was nothing about me that needed to be fixed. Just like there is nothing about you that is wrong either—except the way we all think about ourselves. And once we embrace and accept what makes us different, those flaws disappear. Lean into what you once thought were your imperfections and watch your past vulnerabilities become your future strengths.

"Life is very interesting... In the end, some of your greatest pains become your greatest strengths."
—Drew Barrymore

Rob — I always saw being gay as a flaw. Something that I needed to hide from myself and the world. The 4 Word Answer not only helped me come out, but it has turned what I hide from the world into the key to my success! —Andy

Queer Eye star Carson Kressley had a similar experience. He didn't come out until after he was cast on the show that changed his life. He went from being embarrassed about being gay to embracing his sexuality and making a living out of it! Being **kind** enough to let go of your past is the key to your future success. You are not a failure because you have previously failed. To fail is something that happens to everyone. It is as simple as that. Do not make a failure into a personality trait because failure does not define you unless you let it. Joan Rivers once told me, *"I'm 75 and still being rejected. But you can't get hit by lightning if you don't stand in the rain. No one's been standing in the rain longer than me."* That was the secret to Joan's success. She never gave up and never let what happened yesterday affect what happens today. Joan would stand in the rain longer than anyone. As failure kept pouring down on her, she kept going, knowing the road to success is paved with past failures. Never forget that you only need one yes!

*"There can be a hundred people in the room, and
99 don't believe in you, but one does."*

—Lady Gaga

Learn from your mistakes by thinking about what went wrong and what you could do differently next time, but don't let them consume you. I have failed so many times in so many different areas of my life—business, personal, and even at the beginning of my relationship with my wire fox terrier puppy, Darby—he was crazy hard to housebreak. (I got his permission to reveal this mortifying fact!) Failure feels horrible and embarrassing. There is no way to sugarcoat it, but it needs to happen to teach you the lessons you learn to get you to where you want to go. No one else can do it for you. Let me repeat, no shining armor-clad knight on a horse is coming to save you. Only you can do the work for you to succeed. So, find a safe place where you can practice, fail, succeed, and be ready when opportunity knocks.

"Try and fail, but never fail to try."

—Jared Leto

Hi Rob, my name is Pippa, and I'm a big fan of your podcast and love when you tell us to "do the work." I went back to night school and got my degree, and I start a new job next week. I did the work on myself knowing only I had the power to make this happen. You are an inspiration! #4WA

One of Ashlee Simpson's first performances live on national TV was on *SNL*. Big mistake! She hadn't paid her dues. Ashlee needed to learn her craft by playing every dive piano bar in town like Barry Manilow and Alicia Keys did. Long before Jennifer Lopez shook her bedazzled bottom at Madison Square Garden, she was a backup dancer, lost in the shadows, learning the tools of her trade. My success didn't come overnight. It took me years of learning and watching and practicing before I got my own column and hit podcast. The only person who will determine your successes of tomorrow is you! Instead of being overwhelmed and scared, be inspired, knowing that your success is in no one's hands but your own.

See, the only thing about yourself that was broken was the way you have been thinking about yourself—not you.

When You Are Kind to Yourself, This Happens!

No one, including you, has many "real" friends. Rather, what we do have is lots of people that we know, and there is nothing wrong with acknowledging it. Instead of pretending that everyone you have ever met in your life is your best friend and loves you, focus on the people around you who really matter, especially the most important friend you will ever have—yourself.

> *"Put yourself first. Self-love is not selfish at all. It means that you're taking care of yourself, and like my mom reinforced to me, to make sure that I was safe and that I was healthy."*
> —Laurie Hernandez

It's amazing how many people come in and out of our lives. We start our lives with just family members, then go on to school friends and eventually work and hobby relationships when we become adults. Add to that all the random people from the neighborhood and romantic partners, and all of a sudden, you have a web of many different types of acquaintances. Be honest with yourself about where and how all these people fit in your life. Think about the sliding, ever-changing scales of friendship. From a total stranger to the best friend you will ever have—that person is you! Accept the natural ebb and flow of relationships, knowing that the only thing all these different connections have in common is you! You are the center of your world and the foundation on which every other relationship you have is based. This is why you must treat yourself with **kindness**!

> *"If you're not someone who has a natural and effortless love for yourself, it's hard to let go of your desire to please other people, and that's really not an ingredient for a happy life."*
> —Anne Hathaway

Think of yourself as a spider at the center of the web that is your life. Or a stone dropped into a puddle of water, causing ripples of friendship to spread out from you. Your phone is full of people from every level of friendship because you are the glue that holds all these relationships together. This is why you are responsible for setting the tone of all the interactions in your life. Be **kind** to yourself, and **kindness** will surround you.

"When you take care of yourself, you're a better person for others. When you feel good about yourself, you treat others better."

—Solange

Just like Margaret.

> *I made the conscious decision to be* **kind** *to myself all day, every day. I have now set the bar very high on the way I need to be treated, and miraculously, the people who were meant to be in my life have all risen to the occasion. When I was cruel, I attracted cruel people. When I was* **kind**...*you know the rest because you wrote it! #4WA.*

The secret to having the greatest circle of friends starts with you. It is that simple. I have a small inner circle of friends, and each week, I make sure I check in with all of them. Get into the habit of being involved in the lives of people you love on a regular basis. Send a **kind** text or email to every one of them each week. Don't miss out on the unimportant daily news of their lives because what is insignificant today will be vital tomorrow. Be curious and interested in your squad. Ask questions and listen to the answers because a little bit of effort on your part will produce a massive wave of love that soaks you with love in response. Relationships start as seeds that grow and grow under the right conditions. Make sure you are providing the environment for this to happen.

"I have insecurities of course, but I don't hang out with anyone who points them out to me."

—Adele

It might sound crazy at first, but I have gotten into the routine of checking in with myself as well as my friends. Sending myself a **kind** message each night before I go to bed that I read every morning when I wake up. It doesn't have to be anything poetic or dazzlingly smart and witty because the truth is that nothing you can say is as important as the simple act of saying it. Communicate **kindness**, especially to yourself, and watch your garden of friendship blossom. Like everything else that is important in your life, you have to do the work if you want to see great results. This is exactly what Kim has been doing.

> If I can spend hours each week watching The Kardashians and The Real Housewives, then I can spend time each week with my real pals. I also started putting more effort into the relationship I have with myself. Waking up each morning to a **kind** note that I have sent to myself changes my entire day, and life. You are right: 4WA totally works! KIM.

Don't you feel great when someone reaches out to you for no other reason than to say "hello" and connect? It's a superpower we all have in the palm of our hand. The entire world (including my eighty-five-year-old mother) now has the ability to send a little message of **kindness** without having to open their mouths. Replace the passive aggression, anger, and misery around you with love and **kindness**, and you will change the world. Don't take my word for it, or Kim's—give it a try yourself. What do you have to lose? I can tell you what you have to gain. When you are **kind** to yourself, it makes you the type of person who is **kind** to others. And when you are **kind** to others, you will develop relationships that you never dreamed possible.

> *"As women, we have to start appreciating our own worth and each other's worth. Seek out strong women to befriend, to align yourself with, to learn from, to collaborate with, to be inspired by, to support, and be enlightened by."*
>
> —Madonna

How to Stop Cruel Old Habits from Returning

The reason we give up on those summer diets, the big plans to change our lives, and the New Year's resolutions is that it is much easier to go back to living the old way than to make a change. Change is hard, and the minute our focus shifts, naughty old habits come rushing back. We are all creatures of habit, designed to find comfort in our daily routines, which is why, before long (without putting up much of a fight at all), the new game is over and our old behavior wins. Your gym membership expires, you forget what a vegetable even looks like, and you would rather stay home and watch TV than make an effort to get dressed and go out! This is why we must remain focused and alert. If you don't want to drift back into your old ways, you cannot allow your mind to drift. Remind yourself every day that you are making a choice, and if you are not choosing it, you are not changing it.

"I think in life you should work on yourself until the day you die."

—Serena Williams

Making no decision at all is actually making a big choice. You are choosing to sit on the couch rather than go for a walk. You are choosing to scroll through Instagram rather than text a pal you have not seen in a while. And you are choosing to eat junk food instead of something that will nourish your body. The only one with the power to decide to change your life or to continue with the status quo is you. Behavior, good and bad, begins with the choices you make every day.

"By nature, I keep moving, man. My theory is, be the shark. You've just got to keep moving. You can't stop."

—Brad Pitt

So, don't wait until New Year's Eve to start over, don't wait for summer to get that beach body, and don't wait for tomorrow to go after your dream every day. Be like Doris and do it today. Before *The 4 Word Answer*, Doris would make endless to-do lists and endless excuses to do them tomorrow. Of course, tomorrow never came. Now, the excuses have been replaced by action. And Doris is earning $1,000 extra each month and gets in 4,000+ steps each day.

> I listened to your podcast, and you told me to just do it—well I did, and now everything on my to-do list is crossed off. Doris

I think of my life as a TV show, broken down into hour-long episodes. As a new hour begins, so does a new episode. This little trick has ensured that I no longer procrastinate for very long. Each new hour is a new beginning. The ruts I used to fall into throughout the day now don't last longer than sixty minutes! When you make the decision to reset your life every hour, you give yourself so many more chances to make sure old habits don't win. Refocus at the top of every hour each day and see just how much you will accomplish.

> *"It's never too late—never too late to start over, never too late to be happy."*
> —Jane Fonda

Ken turns the page every hour as the clock chimes, and it has paid off big time for him!

It is easy to get tired and disheartened, which is why starting fresh at the top of each hour has changed my life. Now I'm 45% over this month's target in sales and on track to become Employee of the Month. Ken.

Attack each hour with the same enthusiasm you attack the beginning of each day. Remember—when you change your decisions, you change your life. No one else is coming to do it for you, so stay focused, and stop those cruel old habits from creeping back and taking over. Remember, the only person you need to make sure you don't disappoint is yourself.

"All those things that you're worried about are not important. You're going to be ok. Better than ok. You're going to be great. Spend less time tearing yourself apart, worrying if you're good enough. You are good enough. And you're going to meet amazing people in your life who will help you and love you."
—Reese Witherspoon

We have a choice about what we do and don't do every single day. Choosing to be **kind**, for whatever reason, will change your life, because **kindness** and success are not just linked, they are intertwined. Without **kindness**, you cannot find success. Without success, it is almost impossible to be **kind**. Real **kindness** is real success. Real success is real **kindness**! So, let's get started working on one of the greatest secrets in life. Success and happiness start with being **kind** to yourself.

*"I think probably **kindness** is my number one attribute in a human being. I'll put it before any of the things like courage, or bravery, or generosity, or anything else... **Kindness**—that simple word. To be kind—it covers everything, to my mind. If you're **kind**, that's it."*
—Roald Dahl

PS: When I finally did meet Brad Pitt backstage at *Good Morning America*, he had skin like me too (wink)!

4

C
H
A
P
T
E
R

You Is Smart!

WHEN I FIRST MET JESSICA SIMPSON, BEFORE SHE BECAME AN official client, I foolishly prejudged her and suspected that she wouldn't be the sharpest stiletto in the closet! But after just a few minutes alone with her, inside her $3,000/night suite at the Ritz Carlton Hotel on Central Park South, it was clear that Jess not only knew the difference between chicken and tuna, but she also knew exactly what was going on. Despite what you might have seen on her TV show, Jessica Simpson was certainly no dumb blonde.

> *"I don't have anything to prove anymore. What other people think of me is not my business."*
> —Jessica Simpson

I ended up working with Jess (or Angela, the code name she was **smart** enough to ask her friends to use when she was out in public in disguise) during the peak of her troubled marriage, which America had become so deeply invested in. It became clear very quickly that America's Sweetheart didn't belong to her large TV audience; Jessica Simpson belonged to herself. Labels were important to Jess, not just because she loved shopping and designer clothes, but also because she knew exactly who she was. The girl might have loved her Pucci and her Gucci, yet the label that fit Jessica Simpson best was **smart**—and she had a billion-dollar empire behind her to prove it.

> *"No matter how much money you spend to make yourself beautiful—with all the products, the diets, the plastic surgery—in the end, women need to fall in love with themselves and realize they're wonderfully made."*
>
> —Jessica Simpson

* * *

However, being **smart** and having the confidence to act **smart** are two very different things, and Jessica had the battle scars to show for both. Early on in her career, the music business had only one prototype for every young girl singer: the Britney Spears model. Executive and artist development personnel were all looking for the next Britney, someone who Jessica pretended to be for years, spending too much time doing a poor imitation, rather than being a great version of herself. When that didn't work, Jessica didn't give up. No, she took the only real chance that any of us ever have at finding success. Jessica decided to be herself.

"I should have thought of that a long time ago. It feels good to have success come from what's actually inside of you," Jessica later said as her career soared!

The **smartest** decision you will ever make is deciding to embrace whoever you are, no matter who that might be. Work at being the best you, because pretending to be someone else not only never works out, it makes you miserable. Instead, find out who you are and learn to love and accept that person, because no matter who other people want you to be, you have to be **smart** enough to be you.

"Be original. The world will try to fit you into a mold, but carve your own path."
—Jessica Simpson

Being **smart** was something I didn't think about very much before meeting Jessica Simpson. I grew up being taught that only well-educated people were **smart**. I wanted to do well in school and tried to listen and learn, but with grades well below average, I become quite certain that I was stupid. After my arm was so badly damaged by a metal forceps delivery at birth, I spent my time in the hospital with doctors trying to save it, rather than in the classroom trying to learn. It wasn't until I was eight years old that it was discovered I couldn't read! No wonder I concluded at a very young age that I would have to settle for whatever limited opportunity came my way. I totally believed that people in power—parents, teachers, and my boss at my first job at the bank, where I worked as a teller after leaving school at sixteen years old—were all in charge because they were **smarter** than me. It wasn't until much later in life, after spending so much time with Jessica Simpson—someone who also left school at the ripe old age of sixteen—that I realized how mistaken I had been. Being **smart** and being educated are two totally different things. It took the **smartest** person I have ever met—Jessica Simpson— to teach me that!

> *"Every tear should live its purpose. Don't ever wipe the reason away."*
>
> —Jessica Simpson

This isn't a story that is unique to Jessica Simpson. Just like Jess, Ellen DeGeneres dropped out of the University of New Orleans after only one semester to work odd jobs painting houses and selling vacuums while she worked on her comedy. Ted Turner, who revolutionized the TV news business, didn't drop out of college; instead, he was kicked out of Brown University for allegedly having a woman in his dorm room. Even Steve Jobs dropped out of college after only one semester. He ended up pursuing Eastern spiritualism in India before returning to the United States and convincing his friend Steve Wozniak to start a little business with him you might have heard of; it goes by the name of Apple! It might also surprise you that Rachael Ray has no formal training in the culinary arts (I've been a guest on her show many times and she's even nicer in person), and that one of Hollywood's richest men, David Geffen, who founded or co-founded DreamWorks and Geffen Records, started in the mailroom of the William Morris talent agency. Kourtney and Rob Kardashian are the only ones in the Kardashian/Jenner clan who graduated college, and the list goes on and on. So, clearly, it isn't education that made all these people **smart**! So, what is it?

"Dumb is just not knowing. Ditzy is having the courage to ask!"

—Jessica Simpson

And boy, did Jess have the courage to ask! In fact, I have never met anyone who asks as many questions as she. Jessica surrounds herself with the best and brightest. She isn't scared to admit when she doesn't know the answer and has the confidence to follow her head when she does. Jess loves to debate and disagree and can't stand being told yes when she's wrong. She is perfectly comfortable in her own skin and enjoying learning something new.

What makes Jessica Simpson, Ellen DeGeneres, Ted Turner, Steve Jobs, Rachael Ray, David Geffen, and Kourtney and Rob Kardashian (and every other super successful person I have ever met) **smart** is something you don't learn in a classroom, but rather in life—the most important lesson of believing in yourself. To be clear, I'm not dismissing formal education, but what I am saying is don't be fooled, as I once was, into thinking you need to have gone to a fancy school in order to be **smart** and successful. Like the Scarecrow in *The Wizard of Oz*, it turns out that you, my friend, were **smart** all along. All you needed was Dorothy (or, in my case, Jessica) to point it out. So, let's put on our ruby slippers, click those heels together, and get started working on one of life's four most important lessons: believing that you are **smart**!

This Is Why You Don't Feel Smart

The most foolish thing I ever did was spend too much time be-lieving that being really **smart** was a personality trait, a magic quality that you were either lucky enough to be born with or not. I totally bought into the theory that being **smart** was a God-given gift, something in your DNA, and therefore something that nature had decided, long before we had any say in the matter! This was seemingly confirmed by teachers and test results and, ultimately, me. And resulted in years struggling with anxiety, fear, and constant feelings of failure as I accepted that I wasn't good enough and there was nothing I could do about it. Making stupid choices became a self-fulfilling prophecy because when you feel insecure you are in no position to succeed. Rather, ultimately you do the worst thing a person could ever do to themselves: you stop trying. This was what happened to me. I was at a point in life where I felt so stupid and so worthless that I disappeared into the shadows and let life happen around me.

> *"Twenty years from now you will be more disappointed by the things that you didn't do than by the ones you did do, so throw off the bowlines, sail away from safe harbor, catch the trade winds in your sails. Explore, Dream, Discover."*
> —Mark Twain

Which is exactly what I did once I stopped believing the big fat stupid lie that we are either born **smart** or we are not. Instead, I chose to focus on the truth that the way I had been thinking about the concept of being **smart** was a lie. Something that Alan in Ohio has discovered, too.

*I just registered for classes in business. The thought of being a freshman at 52 years old is terrifying, but I'm doing it anyway, because I might not be educated, but it took me 52 years to believe I am **smart**. I'm **smart** enough to know that it might take me a little longer than my classmates to understand all the complex theories, but I will, and I am going to keep trying, no matter how many times I fail. Because Alan IS good enough. Thanks.*

Yes, you are! Alan knew that if he was ever going to find real happiness and success, he had no choice but to force himself to come up with a new definition of **smart**, and you must do the same. We all need a brand-new revolutionary way of thinking about this topic because the only thing that makes anyone **smart**, really **smart**, is their willingness to try. The fear of trying something new never totally goes away, but putting yourself back out there, knowing you might fail again, is the only chance you have to succeed. Get used to feeling vulnerable and frightened when you go after something new. Neither fear nor failure ever completely disappears, but you can't let them stop you from making the **smartest** decision you will ever make: to get back up and give it another try.

> *"I always did something I was a little not ready to do. I think that's how you grow. When there's that moment of 'Wow, I'm not really sure I can do this,' and you push through those moments, that's when you have a breakthrough."*
>
> —Marissa Mayer

Smart people fail all the time. Jessica Simpson has certainly had her fair share of failure, and she did it with the whole world watching and judging! But because Jess kept going and never gave up, she has also had an extraordinary amount of success. That is the entire point. The two are related. The only way to guarantee neither is to do nothing.

> *"There is only one way to avoid criticism: do nothing, say nothing, and be nothing."*
> —Aristotle

Smart people don't care what people say or think when they don't succeed; they only care about what they themselves say and think. They know that not everyone will like them and they're fine with it. So, the next time you fail, be **smart**, get back up, and remember the true definition of being super **smart** is to keep trying.

> *"I've missed more than 9000 shots in my career. I've lost almost 300 games. 26 times I've been trusted to take the game-winning shot and missed. I've failed over and over and over again in my life. And that is why I succeed."*
> —Michael Jordan

You have to make a choice between courage or comfort, but you cannot choose both. Choosing comfort is the much easier option. It's often dismissed as being lazy, but that is not true. It is not because you are lazy that you choose to live in your comfort zone; it is because you are frightened. It is very scary to keep pushing forward, not knowing the outcome, or to start something completely new that you have never done before. It feels much less risky to do nothing, to overthink a new opportunity to the point where you end up talking yourself out of taking any action at all. You might even convince yourself you are making an intelligent choice avoiding any criticism or risk; however, doubting yourself is not a smart decision. It's a safe one. Don't kid yourself otherwise. Instead, seizing the moment, pushing yourself forward, rejecting fear and excuses, and believing in yourself—that is the **smart** choice.

> *"Do the one thing you think you cannot do. Fail at it. Try again. Do better the second time. The only people who never tumble are those who never mount the high wire. This is your moment. Own it."*
> —Oprah Winfrey

ROB, darn your 4WA! I finally found the courage to apply for the management program at work, and you won't believe it—I GOT ACCEPTED!!!! It is super scary, and I might have diarrhea, but I'm pushing through the terror that has stopped me from doing so many times in the past—and instead, I am believing in me! Colleen

Good for you, Colleen. Learn from the mistakes so you don't make them again, but don't worry. Having enough courage to start means you are already a winner! Learning from your past is essential for a brighter today and tomorrow. Who hasn't promised themselves that they will never do that stupid thing again, and then done exactly that? I know I have! It's because changing behavior that doesn't serve you well is really hard, but it is not impossible. First, you must acknowledge what you did wrong and stop blaming others for it. The best thing to do when you make a bad decision is to own it. Until you can admit out loud that you messed up, you won't change. Then you must move on. Don't dwell on the problem. Focus on the solution. Beating yourself up never helps as it doesn't change anything, and it certainly doesn't put you in the best position to succeed. Neither does relying on willpower alone. What you need to move forward is a clear plan, detailing a different approach that will lead you to a better result. Progress is all about increasing your chances of success and decreasing your chances of failure. That starts with you trusting you are **smart** enough to do this.

> *"You can't connect the dots looking forward; you can only connect them looking backward. So, you have to trust that the dots will somehow connect in your future. You have to trust in something—your gut, destiny, life, karma, whatever. This approach has never let me down, and it has made all the difference in my life."*
>
> —Steve Jobs

You cannot change the people around you, but you can change the people you choose to be around. Behavior is more contagious than singing along to my husband's fabulous hit song, "Copacabana!" If you really want to change your life, you must change the people in it. If you want to be healthier, hang out with people who exercise more and are aware of what they eat and drink. If you want to get better grades, hang out with people who study more. If you want to be happier, say goodbye to the negative people around you, and if you want to be **smart**, find friends who are willing to keep trying despite any setbacks. In Chicago, Randall is ready to start living again after ending a long-term relationship.

> I had let far too many negative people surround me for years. People that pulled me down rather than building me up. Now, I'm making **smart** choices every day. I joined a local amateur theater group and have met some great and dramatic-in-a-good-way people. I've also started to begin going for a walk again each day. These few simple changes have opened paths and stages in my life that had been closed for years. Randall

You can do the same. All it takes is you realizing that you are **smart**. Find people who don't care what others say. Surround yourself with friends who realize not everyone is going to like them. Get that squad that chooses courage over comfort, and embrace those pals who find solutions rather than blaming others. Like Randall, when I started to hang out with people who believe in themselves and me, people who are kind to themselves and me, and folks who even enjoy eating and sharing the occasional vegetable or two—you guessed it, I started to believe in myself, too. I became kinder to myself, and I finally chose to believe that I was **smart**!

> *"It is our choices that show what we truly are, far more than our abilities."*
>
> —J. K. Rowling

It's Smart to Think about
Winning, Not Losing

One positive thought at a time is the only way to win the game of life. Hopefully, it is a game we are all playing for a very long time, so don't be in too much of a rush. Slow down, take a breath, live each moment to its fullest, and learn the rules! To get the best results, you need to start playing with a clear head. You wouldn't expect to win a game of tennis or even cards when you're feeling down, negative, and exhausted. So how do you expect to win the most important game you will ever play without clarity? I have played both ways, with a negative and a positive mental game. And trust me, the latter is much better. We all know what it is like to be in a bad place, a place where it is hard to believe that things will ever get better. And they won't if you are waiting for someone to save you. Instead, be your solution and start thinking about winning, not failing.

"Change will not come if we wait for some other person or some other time. We are the ones we've been waiting for. We are the change that we seek."
—Barack Obama

Bruce L knows this only too well.

I had been thinking of starting my own hair salon for decades. Literally decades, waiting for someone else to do it for me and always thinking of everything that could go wrong. That negative voice kept stopping me until I used The 4 Word Answer and turned to action. And it all started with just one positive thought! Bruce L

I was failing for a long time at the game of life. I knew I needed to make big changes, but I didn't know what those changes should be—that is, until I allowed myself to start thinking about winning, not losing. Playing a bad hand can be made better by making winning choices. Reject that negative voice inside your head. You know the one that plants horrible thoughts, nasty lies, overstays their welcome, and never shuts up! Arm yourself with a positive mental game so that the moment you hear those negative voices coming, you can slam the door shut on them. Close the windows too, because negativity is all around us all the time. You won't even notice it until you start thinking about winning. Then will you discover that just like in the horror movies, the most dangerous voices are coming from inside the house!

> *"No one will take care of you if you don't take care of yourself."*
> —Alicia Keys

Get into the habit of playing what I like to call the "positive mind game" all day long. The rules are simple: you just need to challenge yourself to be more positive in every aspect of your life by considering the endless solutions rather than the mounting problems. For example, my dog Darby needs to go for a walk every morning around 6:30 AM! Moving his dinner back an hour pushed this to 7:30 AM, which still was an hour before Daddy likes to get out of bed; however, after months of moaning that there is no snooze button on a dog, I started to play the "positive mind game" and transformed the negative into a positive. Now, walking down 24th Street as the city begins to wake up and stretch is actually rather amazing. I have gotten to meet other people in my building who I had never met before and have ended up becoming friendly with my neighbor and his beautiful standard poodle! Plus, I get an extra hour each morning to focus on myself before my phone starts blowing up with the world's breaking celebrity gossip pouring in. It was during those extra sixty minutes each day that I finally got to finish this book. I've come to see my mornings as a blessing, living in a city I adore, knowing unconditional love from my boy Darby. I'm slightly embarrassed to admit that after all these years thinking otherwise, I'm actually a morning person! And it's all because I chose to look at doing exactly the same task in a totally different, positive way. Change the way you think, and you will change your life!

> *"The optimist sees the donut; the pessimist sees the hole."*
>
> —Oscar Wilde

And although they didn't have a Dunkin' Donuts when I was living in Scotland, Angus knows exactly what we are talking about!

I'm Angus from Glasgow, and with my new attitude and the 4WA, my life has changed for the better in so many ways. I use the positive mind game every single day and give it my best shot. You can always find the silver lining in things I used to moan about, if you try. Even our rainy weather isn't so bad anymore. I'm splashing around the city like I'm the Scottish Gene Kelly in Singing in the Rain!

Angus is absolutely right. If you can't change your situation, you can change your mind—which is exactly what I did a few weeks ago. I jumped into a town car early one morning, feeling grumpy, tired, and overworked. I was heading to *Good Day New York* to talk with everyone's favorite person in morning TV, Rosanna Scotto, about last night's Grammy award winners. There was literally nothing wrong with this picture except my attitude. As we shot up Eighth Avenue in a chauffeur car the show had provided, I put down my notes and looked out the window. It was a beautiful day outside, and I was about to ruin it. I caught myself, and just like that, I stopped, refocused, and thought about winning. Of all the entertainment experts in the world, New York's top morning show wanted me! What was my problem with that?

"Gratitude is the closest thing to beauty manifested in an emotion."
—Mindy Kaling

You can be angry when you get the wrong order at Starbucks or grateful that you can afford an eight-dollar cup of coffee! You can snap back when someone pushes in front of you at the supermarket checkout, or you can shake it off and think about what delicious treats you are going to have for dinner. The point is, **smart** people understand that in a world where circumstances are out of your control, you get to control the way you react. Realize that the small decisions you make every moment add up to define who you are in the long run. Stop getting in the way of your own story and start enjoying what is going on outside your window.

*"There are always flowers for those who want to
see them."*

—Henri Matisse

Here is an exercise to help: see if you can go an entire day
without complaining. I know from experience that it is harder
than it sounds. Write down every single time you complain in
twenty-four hours, and I promise you that by the time you go to
bed, you will complain one more time about how long the list is!
Mine was over one hundred, and that was on what I considered
to be a good day! Think about it, if every complaint is just sixty
seconds long, when you complain one hundred times a day, one
hour and forty minutes are wasted on evading responsibility
instead of finding a solution every single day.

*"You don't really have a problem if the problem can
be solved with doing something about it."*

—Jessica Simpson

Lenny was shocked when she became aware of how many
times a day she moaned!

> Rob, I was horrified at the amount of time I wasted
> complaining. I didn't even know I was doing it until I
> started to write it down. I'm too embarrassed to give
> you a number, but let's just say, you are an amateur
> with only 100! The first step is noticing and then stop-
> ping it. I am now focused on winning, not losing. #moti-
> vation #winning

I remember being invited to a book party for David Zinczenko at the Dream Hotel on 16th Street in New York City. David has made an entire career out of the *Eat This, Not That* franchise that he had created and was celebrating another tome within his expanding empire. We knew each other professionally from appearing on the same daytime TV circuit, but we were not close friends. Plus, a pal of mine from NBC had slept with him while they were both working at the Olympics in Beijing. It turns out that Mr. Six-Pack spent more time admiring himself in the mirror than touching "this and not that" in the bedroom! Yet, despite Dave's poor review, he has a boyish charm, and he certainly knew how to sell books! Later that evening, when I found myself standing alone in the bathroom, holding his book in my hand, I realized the secret to his success.

Dave was successful, not because he was telling us what we should and shouldn't eat, but rather, because he was identifying a problem and offering a solution. Replacing the bad with the good in one easy serving was a brilliant idea. Inspired, I realized that is exactly what we need to be doing with the way we think. The next time you have a negative thought, replace it with a positive one. Pull that sucker out like a weed before it takes root, and just as importantly, fill the hole it leaves behind with a rose! It's not enough to just get rid of the bad. We need to replace it with something good. Think this, not that. Think winning, not losing!

"Once you replace negative thoughts with positive ones, you'll start having positive results."
—Willie Nelson

You Decide the Moment to Start Over

Start thinking about your life like it is a book. It has an unmistakable beginning, a definite end, and lots of chapters in between. Some are long, and some are short. Some are interesting, and some are dull. There might even be a few chapters that blend together or repeat themselves over and over again. When you think about your life like this, it reminds you that the author of this great adventure is you! Only *you* have the power to decide when a new chapter starts and when an old chapter ends. It's your life, so if you find yourself in the wrong story or not enjoying the plot, change it. Never forget that you get to decide if you are going to play the victim or the hero.

> *"No matter who you are, no matter what you did, no matter where you've come from, you can always change, become a better version of yourself."*
> —Madonna

Remember that there are hundreds of ways to reach a goal, so don't get stuck reliving the same story and expecting a different ending. Hoping to get somewhere new by doing the same thing isn't going to happen. Instead, embrace change and keep on trying when your first, second, third, and maybe even more plans don't work. The biggest mistake people make is giving up—don't! Change your plan, but not your goal, and when things don't work out and come to an end, be **smart** and admit it. Watering dead plants is exhausting, and it never brings them back to life. Instead, close that chapter and start a new one.

"Survival can be summed up in three words—never give up. That's the heart of it really. Just keep trying."

—Bear Grylls

> Hi ROB! Your 4WA really was the answer to all the problems in my personal and professional life. Learning to move on and walk away has been game-changing for me. I was always the last one to leave the party, which was never a good look. I kept holding on to so many things in my life well past their expiration dates. I stayed in a horrible job and an even worse personal relationship for way too long. I wouldn't have been able to let go without the 4WA. I've just changed jobs, and I love what I'm doing now. For the first time in my life, I am engaged, and he is great. None of this would have happened had I not closed a chapter and moved on! Debbie

If you want to make real changes in your life, just like Debbie, you have to change your habits. Don't be afraid of finding a new route that is going to get you to your goal. You have to start being totally honest with yourself. You deserve to be in a relationship where you are safe to say uncomfortable things. Every relationship in your life will be stronger when you tell the truth, especially when you are honest with yourself. If the truth leads to breakups, to the end of a chapter in your life, even breaks your heart, in the long run, you will live a much better life because of it.

"Truth is like the sun. You can shut it out for a time, but it ain't goin' away."

—Elvis Presley

Focus on taking one small step at a time. Think about the one thing you can do right now—then do it! Don't think about running a marathon, think about taking the first step. Writing a book starts with a single sentence. You are not going to lose one hundred pounds until you shed the first one. Don't overwhelm yourself worrying about tomorrow; think about what you can do today. Be patient knowing that big things happen when you make small decisions, not big ones.

"You don't have to see the whole staircase, just take the first step."

—Martin Luther King Jr.

The 4 Word Answer was started after I was inspired by a movie but finished after I worked on it every day for just thirty minutes. That's it. I found half an hour, in two fifteen-minute intervals, seven days a week, where I disappeared into a quiet corner of my apartment or walked down to the river and found an empty bench under a tree and did the work, knowing that what I did today would mean I would finish one day sooner. What kept me going was not biting off more than I could chew, never overwhelming myself with the enormity of the task at hand, and being **smart** enough to believe in myself!

"Every professional was once an amateur."

—Nike

Every night before you go to bed, write down one thing that you are going to accomplish the next day, one small task that will get you closer to your final goal. This approach has changed my life! Doing this each day has not only transformed my productivity level, but it has also increased my level of happiness because nothing feels better than getting it done. When you are disciplined and focus on the next fifteen minutes, the next fifteen years will take care of themselves. Take a deep breath and think about the one thing you are going to start today!

> *"Respect your efforts, respect yourself. Self-respect leads to self-discipline. When you have both firmly under your belt, that's real power."*
> —Clint Eastwood

For years, I tried to do everything and ended up doing nothing. My life was littered with half-finished projects and hard-assed relationships. The day I started the 4WA was the day everything changed. For just 30 minutes a day, I had the discipline and focus to work on one task. When I completed it, I moved onto the next. After just a few months, my life has been transformed. Thank you, Pippa

The next time you are having a bad day, remember that a bad moment is simply that, a moment! Ask yourself, are you really having a bad day or was it just a bad moment that you turned into a bad day by obsessing about it? When you fight with your partner or kids or parents, when you get cut off in traffic or miss your train, when you get the wrong coffee as you're rushing to the office, you get to choose if you are going to dwell on it for the entire day or move on. You only have a bad day when you choose to have one!

> *"Cry me a river, build a bridge, and get over it."*
> —Justin Timberlake

If whatever is wrong isn't going to matter four minutes, four days, or four years from now, why are you refusing to say goodbye to it? Be like Beyoncé, find the good in goodbye, and never forget that you have the power, and the right, to decide when to start over—like right now!

> *"What we call the beginning is often the end. And to make an end is to make a beginning. The end is where we start from."*
> —T.S. Eliot

Every Smart Person Sets a Deadline

How often do you put off doing something that makes you feel uncomfortable? Saying "I will do it tomorrow" is the easiest way to make sure nothing ever happens. I know it's a lot easier to say, "I'll do it tomorrow," but tomorrow never comes unless you set a deadline and stick to it. No one knows this better than I do after a decade of putting things off and pushing away my dreams. All that changed when I started being honest with myself about the real reason that I was doing this—I was scared. Frightened to go after my dreams, it felt safer to convince myself that I would get around to it one day, rather than letting today be day one of getting it done.

> *"Only put off until tomorrow what you are willing to die having left undone."*
> —Pablo Picasso

When it comes to getting stuff done, you have two options: excuses or changes! It is that simple. Excuses are just your fears, desperately hoping to convince you not to do anything new. Keeping you in your comfort zone, in a place that feels familiar; however, you are never too busy, too old, too fat, too stupid, or too anything to make a change. What you are is making excuses because you are frightened! The next time you make an excuse, admit that you are scared; then set a deadline.

> *"There will be many times in your life—at school, and more particularly when you are a grown-up— when people will distract or divert you from what needs to be done. You may even welcome the distraction. But if you use it as an excuse for not doing what you are supposed to do, you can blame no one but yourself. If you truly wish to accomplish something, you should allow nothing to stop you, and chances are you'll succeed."*
> —Julie Andrews

Learning this changed Rachel's life.

> Hi Rob, I used to let myself get distracted by other people all the time. When other people were not around, I would distract myself. Now I understand that I was looking for excuses because I was scared. I didn't think I deserved a good life and lived in fear that one day I would be exposed as a fraud until I found The 4 Word Answer. Now, I know I deserve a great life and won't let anyone, including myself, sabotage it. Don't be scared, be **smart**! Rachel

We can all learn a lesson from Rachel. When we are honest with ourselves, our fears don't disappear, but our excuses do. Push forward. Even if your legs are shaking, keep walking. Even if your voice is trembling with fear, speak up and refuse to be silenced. Don't forget that you are **smart** and brave enough to go after all your dreams.

> *"The biggest risk is not taking any risk. In a world that is changing really quickly, the only strategy that is guaranteed to fail is not taking risks."*
> —Mark Zuckerberg

Smart people are never too busy to make the time to do what is important. They don't cloak themselves in excuses to stop themselves from doing anything new. Rather, they opt for an extraordinary life, not a safe one. You have to take chances, or you will never grow. And if you never grow because you keep making excuses, you will regret it.

"Your regrets aren't what you did, but what you didn't do. So, I take every opportunity."
—Cameron Diaz

Procrastination is not who you are; it is what you do. To procrastinate is not in your DNA. It is not your natural state of being, and it is not something that was God-given to you. No one is a born procrastinator. Rather, some have a bad habit of procrastinating. To break it, write down all the things you don't want to do today: the phone calls you want to ignore, the emails you don't want to respond to, the conversations you don't want to have, and the tasks that you have been putting off forever. Now, start with the one thing you want to do the least. Get it out of the way and out of your mind. The very last person I want to speak to is the person I call first. The thing I want to avoid the most is the first thing I get done each morning. It does not matter if you start scared or late or even start over—you just need to start. Once you do, you will discover that the best way to silence fear is to begin.

"There are two basic motivating forces: fear and love. When we are afraid, we pull back from life. When we are in love, we open to all that life has to offer with passion, excitement, and acceptance. We need to learn to love ourselves first, in all our glory and our imperfections. If we cannot love ourselves, we cannot fully open to our ability to love others or our potential to create. Evolution and all hopes for a better world rest in the fearlessness and open-hearted vision of people who embrace life."
—John Lennon

*My name is Jenna, and I feel like half my life has been stolen by procrastinating. I was the queen of putting off everything. From little stuff, like doing my laundry, to big stuff that has affected my job and my health. It was all about how I wasn't **smart** enough to admit I was full of fear. Things got so bad that I had to choose. I chose to get off my butt and get to work on time in clean clothes and set a deadline and to be smart enough to love myself. The [4 Word] Answer has given me my life back. I can never thank you enough. —Jenna*

Like Jenna, take a deep breath and have faith in yourself. Every lesson. Every challenge. Every hard moment. Everything you are learning along the way all happened to get you where you need to go. Remember why you don't feel **smart**. Think about winning, not failing. Don't forget that you decide when to start over, and always set a deadline. Finally, like Jessica Simpson, never give up. You is **smart**—and don't you ever forget it!

*"The sexiest thing in the entire world is being really **smart**. And being thoughtful. And being generous. Everything else is crap! I promise you! It's just crap that people try to sell to you to make you feel like less. So, don't buy it. Be **smart**, be thoughtful, and be generous."*

—Ashton Kutcher

You Is Important!

IT IS SMART TO BE KIND. IT IS KIND TO TREAT PEOPLE LIKE they are smart. And it's both smart and kind to believe that everyone, but especially you, is **important**.

I worked for years with P. Diddy as his publicist—going through more name changes and drama than I can remember. Puff Daddy, Puffy, P. Diddy, Diddy, or Sean. (Spot the odd one out!) He ran a marathon. He starred in a Broadway play. He flew around the country in a private jet with Leonardo DiCaprio trying to get people to vote. He sold t-shirts. He sold vodka. He hosted MTV's Video Music Awards in Miami during a hurricane. And he even ran a record company in his spare time.

"It always seems impossible until it's done."
—Diddy

Puff is the modern-day PT Barnum. A rare Renaissance man who knows how to put on a show wherever he goes. He was the inspiration for his then-girlfriend Jennifer Lopez to rename herself JLo—shorter names make signing autographs much easier! He was one of the first stars to embrace, rather than hide from, celebrity endorsements, and he made history in 1993 when he started his own company, Bad Boy Entertainment. Puff was infectious to be around, possessing what his team would joke were his "Puff the Magic Dragon" qualities. All of this was possible because Puff believed he was **important**. And because he believed it, it became true!

Puff was born with every disadvantage you need if you are going to succeed! He was born and raised in Harlem by his magnificent single mother after his father was murdered. Mamma Combs, as we would all call her, taught her son at an early age that everyone, including a skinny, black, single-parent kid, had something to contribute. She instilled in her young son that everyone mattered and that if you have a pulse, you have a purpose. Puffy taught me that people aren't quiet. You just haven't found a topic that interests them yet! He understood that no matter your background, wealth, gender, color, or sexuality, once you found a topic you had in common with someone else, you had found a potential new best friend. How else could you explain the unlikely relationships between Puff and Clive Davis, Puff and Ashton Kutcher, Puff and *Vogue* editor Anna Wintour, and even Puff and cosmetic king Leonard Lauder?

> "If you're chasing your dream, you're not running fast enough. Run faster."
>
> —Diddy

From Allison — I have changed my life thanks to Rob Shuter, and we have never even met. You've helped me chase and catch my dream. Since listening to your show, I've lost 37 pounds and reinvigorated my life. I doubt you will ever read this, but it doesn't matter because I had to say thank you for the story you told about your ex-client Puffy. I used to think I was shy and quiet my whole life, until I started to believe I was **important** *enough to chase my dreams. That simple step of believing in myself started a chain of events that has changed my entire life. I believe in me!*

Diane Sawyer once told me, on a flight to Prague to interview my client tsunami-survivor model Petra Nemcova, that everyone treated her like she was **important** because, after all, she is Diane Sawyer; however, it was how people treated the folks around Diane—the makeup team, the producers, the camera and sound crew, and the assistants—that told her *everything* about them. Every successful person understands exactly what Diane is talking about. Not only did Puff know that he was **important**, but he also knew that every single person he ever met was **important** too because one day, at least one of these people would be **important** in his life.

> *"Doesn't matter how educated, talented, rich or cool you believe you are, how you treat people ultimately tells all."*
>
> —Diddy

I remember having a shy guy on my TV show who seemed very uncomfortable being on camera. I went out of my way to make him comfortable, treating him with kindness long before I discovered *The 4 Word Answer*. I had no ulterior motive other than to make him feel welcome on my set full of strangers. This turned out to not only be a kind move, but also a very smart one, because that guy was one of the most **important**, most listened-to radio personalities in America. Sorry, I'm not talking about you, Howard Stern; I'm talking about Z100's amazing Elvis Duran. We became friends, and Elvis became an **important** person in my professional life, partially responsible for me getting my own iHeartRadio show. All this happened because I believed in myself enough to know I could make a difference. I had the power to make a stranger feel **important**, and so, I did!

> *"I was sort of a loner as a kid, so radio was where*
> *I turned for companionship. I loved the music*
> *and how the DJs talked about the artists and used*
> *words to paint pictures to evoke emotion."*
> —Elvis Duran

Think about all the people in your life that you have brushed off in the past—the assistant who got you a cup of coffee who you didn't thank, the receptionist whose name you've still never bothered to learn, or the waiter you snapped at during lunch (all jobs I once held). Every one of these people might one day go on to play an **important** role in your future! Be especially kind when you don't need anyone's help, because the baton of power is constantly changing hands. Life is always rearranging and changing what position we are all in, which is why it is smart to always make everyone feel **important**, especially yourself.

> I didn't realize the power of what I was saying and do- ing. You have taught me just how **important** we all are every day. Treating people with kindness and respect is so smart. Now, coworkers and even strangers want to help me out. When you treat people as you want to be treated and realize how **important** everyone is, life is better! For the first time in my life, I really like my- self!!!! —Robin

That brings us back to the real secret to Puff's success: Puff makes everyone feel indispensable, critical, essential, significant, central, and **important**—because Puff feels **important** himself! When you feel **important**, you become **important**. It is as easy as that. All it takes is a little bit of Puff the Magic Dragon fairy dust and a lot of believing in yourself.

> *"I think that you have to believe. That's one of my biggest mantras—believe. I wouldn't be here if I didn't believe in myself."*
>
> —Diddy

The Most Important Person in Your Life Is YOU

It's impossible to treat anyone else like they are **important** until you believe that *you* are **important**. Only when you value yourself can you understand that your opinions matter the most. Once you know how **important** your opinions are, you will be much more careful sharing them. Start talking to yourself like you are talking to the most **important** person in your life. I wish it was a gift that could be wrapped with a big red bow and handed out every birthday and Christmas, but it doesn't work that way. Believing that you are **important** has to start with you, nobody else. It's not a bad thing, as it puts the power into your hands rather than anyone else's. You, and only you, can walk the long, lonely road to success, so start depending on you.

> *"Your self-worth is determined by you. You don't have to depend on someone telling you who you are."*
> —Beyoncé

I started this journey feeling about as worthless as anyone possibly could feel. But step after step, reminding myself, somewhat unconvincingly at first, that I mattered led me to a better place. I was running a marathon that would take a lifetime to finish, because learning that you are **important** isn't easy. For years, I had been taught the opposite, to the point where I felt selfish finally putting myself first. This is a bad habit that we all need to break because the truth is that each and every one of us is **important** enough to do whatever it takes to take care of ourselves first!

> *"You know what? Especially with women, we are usually the caretakers of everyone except for ourselves. If I don't take care of myself and I'm taking care of my daughter or my husband or*

*whatever—I'm running on fumes. I have nothing
left to give. Nothing. But when I take the time to
take care of myself, go to the doctor, go to a spa, get
a deep-tissue massage, get adjusted by a chiroprac-
tor ... I feel like I can face life with a renewed vigor
and renewed passion."*

—Viola Davis

We all have jobs and chores and lots of things we have to do
in life, but the only way we can do it all and not lose ourselves in
the process is if we believe we are **important**. When you live your
life like you are the most **important** person in it, guilty pleasures
vanish. You will never feel embarrassment or guilt about doing
something you really enjoy ever again. Imagine valuing yourself
so much that you never feel the need to apologize for who you
are, understanding that you have nothing to be sorry for. Once
you believe that you are **important**, you will be free to do the
things that bring you pleasure more often. Postponing even the
smallest of things that let you zone out and make you really
happy will be a thing of the past!

*"It's a way to be creative and experimental without
being extremely physical, which is what I'm used
to. And it's mentally relaxing. There's nothing like
zoning out and chopping onions."*

—Misty Copeland

*When my alarm clock goes off, I start my day by saying the four words out loud. I don't feel guilty or embarrassed anymore taking the time I need for me. I now stop on my way to work and get a healthy, delicious lunch instead of grabbing fast food to eat at my desk and then complaining that I am overweight—because I am worth it. I loved your story about Misty Copeland chopping onions to zone out, my no-longer-guilty pleasure is knitting. I'm working on a winter scarf for you, Rob, after I finish one for the most **important** person in my life—and I'm making no apologies for saying that it is MEEEEEEEEE!"* —Jenney*

It is not arrogant or selfish to know that you are the most **important** person in your life. It doesn't diminish the **importance** of all the other people with whom we all share our lives, including family, friends, coworkers, and even pets. In order for you to treat others with the care and respect they deserve, you have to start caring and respecting yourself first. Remember that loving others is a choice; however, it's not an option when it comes to loving yourself. Acknowledging that you are the most **important** person in your life is the ultimate selfless act. You owe it to yourself to breathe, relax, and take the time to remember that you are **important**.

"After adding everyone's schedule on the calendar, I make sure that every day I have some sacred time for myself, so I can recharge. I noticed that every time I felt overwhelmed, I would hold my breath. I had to learn to stop, relax and take long deep

breaths and within seconds I would feel more clear and ready to deal with the situation in a more loving way. Meditation also has been a wonderful tool. I notice that when I don't take the time to do it, I am not as centered, patient or clear."

—Gisele Bündchen

No one can make you feel unimportant without your consent, so stop allowing unimportant people to make you feel unimportant. You are the boss of your life so be the boss you always wanted to have. This begins with taking responsibility for each and every decision you make and being the **important** force for good in your life and the lives of others. You are much further along on this journey than you think, and the finish line is not too far away.

*"May the Force be with you' is charming but it's not **important**. What's **important** is that you become the Force—for yourself and perhaps for other people."*

—Harrison Ford

By the Time They Support You, You Realize You Never Needed Them!

I used to be one of those people who needed everyone to love and support me. I wasn't happy unless I felt liked by even folks I didn't know. I was so desperate for everyone else's approval that I disappeared. Immobilized by fear of what others might think, I dimmed my own light rather than risk being seen as the real me. Even a comment on my Facebook page had the power to devastate me to the point that I second-guessed every new post. It wasn't just online where I was disappearing; I became invisible in my real life, too. At work, I found myself speaking out less and less and in my private life, I almost stopping getting up off the couch and going out at all. I was censoring myself in order to censor how other people reacted to me. I completely vanished, leaving behind nothing for anyone to like or dislike. Sound familiar?

> *"Your need for acceptance can make you invisible in this world. Don't let anything stand in the way of the light that shines through this form. Risk being seen in all of your glory."*
>
> —Jim Carrey

Trying to win over people who aren't on board is a full-time game that you are guaranteed to lose. If you find yourself quickly swiping by all the people who are supporting you to find the one who didn't, you know you have a problem! Obsessing about that one negative comment all day long while ignoring all the positive ones is a waste of time that you can never get back. Think about it! If you spend just thirty minutes per day thinking about people who disapprove (and we all know it can be much more than thirty minutes!), that adds up to 210 minutes per week! That is 10,920 minutes per year. You are wasting one week of your life every 365 days, all because you don't feel **important** enough to know you don't need them.

> *"I worked with someone who told me they'd never like me. But for some reason, I just felt like I needed*

her approval. So, I started changing myself to please her. It made me stop being social and friendly. I was so unhappy."

—Ariana Grande

> My life is finally moving forward because I no longer need everyone's approval to live. Rob Shuter, you have been haunting me in all the right ways! I am no longer scared. I am **important** enough to just be me, and they can like it or lump it. I have you to thank for showing me that I matter. —Diane

There are many reasons people don't support you, but at the end of the day, it doesn't matter. You are not going to change them, but you can change you! Get rid of the idea that you must please others and start focusing on pleasing the only person who matters—yourself. When you live your life without needing the approval of others, not only do you get back the enormous amount of wasted time, but you also get all those hours to focus on *you* and what you think. This starts by reminding yourself every day that you are **important**. The only person you need to please is yourself. Listen to your instincts and see what happens when you realize that you never needed anyone else!

> *"Once you get rid of the idea that you must please other people before you please yourself, and you begin to follow your own instincts—only then can you be successful. You become more satisfied and*

when you are, other people tend to be satisfied by
what you do."

—Raquel Welch

Watch! Once you no longer need their approval, you will get it. When you learn that there is only an audience of one, others will want a seat to the performance called your life too. By the time they decide to support you, you already have all the support you will ever need from the most **important** person in your world: *you!*

> *"Eventually you just have to realize that you're liv-*
> *ing for an audience of one. I'm not here for anyone*
> *else's approval."*
>
> —Pamela Anderson

When People Don't Like You, Do This!

Why do we hang out with people who don't really like us? And why do we hang out with people we don't really like? The answer is simple: it's because we don't feel **important** enough to stop.

The day I stopped making plans with people who didn't care for me was the day I started hanging out with people who did. You might not believe it at this moment, but there are people out there who will really, really like you. You just haven't found them yet. The reason you haven't found them is that you have been too busy wasting time hanging out with the wrong folks. Look carefully at all the relationships you have in your life and ask yourself, "Do I really enjoy spending time with these people?" When you say goodbye to them and head home, check to see if you have a big fat smile on your face. If not, stop spending so much time with them and start spending more time with people who make you happy.

> *"A day without a friend is like a pot without a single drop of honey left inside."*
>
> —Winnie the Pooh

Rob, I really enjoyed the moment on your show [when you talked] about what to do when people don't really like us—find friends that do! I have never heard anyone say it so clearly. It is so simple and so true. I'm already teaching it to my 9-year-old daughter. So looking forward to seeing my life and her young life change for the better. We are both **important** enough to have real friends and lots of honey, too! —Crystal

Making new friends at any age isn't easy. It's hard to put yourself out there and meet new people. It takes a huge amount of effort with no results guaranteed. And that is why so many of us stop trying. It's much easier to settle into the status quo and socialize with people who really aren't very nice to us. Just because it is easier doesn't make it the right choice. Be bold and brave and believe that you deserve to be surrounded by the best friends in the world. Friends who will inspire you to be the best you can be. Remember, it is better to have just a few friends with whom you completely connect than lots and lots with whom there is no connection at all. You can tell a lot about someone by looking at their friends, but you can tell even more about your friends by looking at you! Demand the best, and that is what you shall have.

"I really believe you are the company you keep, and you have to surround yourself with people who lift you up, because the world knocks you down."
—Maria Shriver

Don't worry if you haven't found your people yet. Your tribe is out there; you have simply been looking in the wrong places. The key to finding new friends is to break up your old routines. Get out of your comfort zone and challenge yourself to try something new. Put yourself in environments where you will meet people with similar interests and passions, because no one is going to discover you sitting alone in your room. Join a club or a group centered around something that you find interesting. Sign up for that class or a course you always wanted to take. Give people a reason, or four, to want to hang out with you and, most **importantly**, be open to making new friends wherever you go. Who knows? You might find a lifelong soulmate the next time you buy a cup of coffee, just as Cameron and Drew did.

"She was 16 and I was 14 when we became friends. We were both LA kids. I worked in a coffeehouse and she was a model. I served her a coffee, and we had mutual friends, and we just knew each other from around town. I will say this about her—she was always kind. Someone who looks like that, they could have an attitude, and she was the opposite. She was friendly and goofy and really nice."
—Drew Barrymore, about her friend Cameron Diaz

THE 4 WORD ANSWER

"She (Drew) has the most amazing heart. She is one of my closest girlfriends, but the way she loves the people around her is really special. She is so giving of herself and so accepting of others. She has created this community for herself. She didn't really have a strong family, so friends are her family. She really loves on that level of just unconditional love. And her friends around her love her in that way as well. She is one big heart, Drew! She doesn't even wear it on her sleeve; it's like she is just a heart."
—Cameron Diaz about her best friend Drew Barrymore (who she met at a coffee shop)

Only when you feel **important** will you find the courage to push the excuses away. Once you do, you will find friends that you never dreamed possible. True pals who always have your back, who stand up and defend you when others try to tear you down. People who will help you without reservation or reward when it is convenient and when it is not. Individuals who are always honest about you in the kindest way possible, who will accept you for being you while encouraging you to become the best version of yourself, whoever that is. Folks who want what's best for you and will never abandon you when times get tough.

"Friendship is the hardest thing in the world to explain. It's not something you learn in school. But if you haven't learned the meaning of friendship, you really haven't learned anything."
—Muhammad Ali

Rejection Is an Important Gift

What if rejection was really a present telling you that whatever you thought you wanted actually wasn't right for you? Because that is exactly what rejection is. It is a gift that doesn't strip away your dreams, but rather leads you toward them. Rejection doesn't have to destroy your self-confidence. Instead, it will build self-confidence and increase your self-worth—if you let it! In fact, everything you have been taught about being told no is the opposite. After yes, the next best answer you can ever hear is no. With both, you are able to move on. It's when you get a maybe that you are left dangling, waiting for a final decision. Don't worry about rejection. Worry about regret!

> *"Failure is an answer. Rejection is an answer. Regret is an eternal question you will never have the answer to."*
>
> —Trevor Noah

I was talking to my friend about all the terrible dates I have been on and was telling her about Rob Shuter and The 4 Word Answer! She was blown away about your entire way of seeing rejection as a gift. It totally makes sense. She said, "Thank God all those losers rejected us. Can you imagine how awful life would have been if they hadn't and we had married them?! Look up a few people who turned you down in the past on Facebook and see what they are doing now.... We dodged a bullet!" —Jennifer

The crush who turned you down that you thought was going to be the love of your life, the job that went to someone less qualified that was going to make you rich and famous, and the school that didn't accept you that was going to change your future—they all did you a massive favor when they told you no because none of them were the right fit for you. No matter how hard you wanted to believe they were, they were not! You were not supposed to be dating that person who didn't want you. That job that hired someone else might have given you a paycheck for a while, but it was never going to make you fulfilled and happy. And you would have been miserable at that school where you were never going to make friends and fit in. Allow yourself to be disappointed in the moment, but know that the future has a soulmate, a career, and an education out there that is perfect for you.

> *"It doesn't feel good in this moment, but in the future, it's the thing that's going to light you up so you can stay lit! When you look at the thing, the deeper the heartache, the more you needed to learn, and that's actually the truth.... Every heartache is there to teach you something about yourself."*
> —Oprah Winfrey

The first guy I thought I had fallen in love with was Craig from Great Barr, Birmingham, England. We would slip out of school together during our lunch breaks to make out in the woods. He was tall with strawberry blonde hair, the head of the school gym team, and had muscles that Chris Hemsworth would have been jealous of! I always thought Craig was way out of my league, but that didn't stop me from spending most of my classes dreaming about how perfect our lives would be together! Then

Craig dumped me and refused to talk to me ever again. That was the first time I remember being rejected and how much it hurt. My dream of doing the perfect forward roll into "happily ever after" was shattered! Although Craig was the first, he certainly wasn't the last rejection I would ever get. The point is, I can't tell you how many times I have felt rejected since Craig, romantically and professionally, but I can tell you exactly how many times I have been rejected since *The 4 Word Answer*—not once! Now a rejection is no longer a no, but rather a yes toward something better for me.

> *"Don't be afraid to fail. It's not the end of the world and in many ways it's the first step toward learning something better and getting better at it."*
> —Jon Hamm

Just so you know, the 4WA is my inspiration. I'm doing so much better because of you. I'm not afraid to fail anymore as every misstep is a step in finding what is right for me. Without fear in my life, I'm on pace to double my business in just over a year, and I have found a prince, which took a lot of kissing frogs! —Britney

Rejection is simply redirection, a gift that pushes you toward the path that was always right for you. Once you understand this, it gets much easier to brush off the hurt and pain of being told no. Instead of reacting cynically, learn to be grateful that you are going in the right direction. When you take the fear out of rejection, you take away its crippling pain and power. Now when someone tells you no, don't get hurt and disappointed, but rather, think of it as a yes. Learn a lesson. Practice acceptance, not rejection. And take off the blindfold to see the truth about the situation.

> *"Cynicism masquerades as wisdom, but it is the furthest thing from it. Because cynics don't learn anything. Because cynicism is a self-imposed blindness: a rejection of the world because we are afraid it will hurt us or disappoint us. Cynics always say 'no.' But saying 'yes' begins things. Saying 'yes' is how things grow."*
>
> —Stephen Colbert

In 1989, an unknown actress appeared on *The Howard Stern Show* to promote the weight loss program Nutrisystem, although Howard was much more interested in her breast size than the size of the portions on her plate. Humiliated and feeling rejected, the actress who had been cast in a few minor shows wasn't sure if her big break was ever going to happen. She was ready to give up. That's when she bumped into Warren Littlefield, the president of NBC Entertainment, at 10:30 PM in a gas station on Sunset Boulevard. "I'm at the Chevron station gassing up, and Jennifer is over at the other island, and she comes over, and she says, 'Is it ever going to happen?' and I say, 'We believe in you. I love you. I so believe in your talent, I'm sure it will.' A few months later, we handed her the Friends script." That actress was Jennifer Aniston, who went on to be one of the highest-paid actresses on TV, earning $1 million per episode of *Friends*.

"I was told to avoid the business altogether because of the rejection. People would say to me, 'Don't you want to have a normal job and a normal family?' I guess that would be good advice for some people, but I wanted to act."

—Jennifer Aniston

On April 1, 1977, the boss at local Baltimore station WJZ-TV pulled the anchor off the evening news and moved her to the dead shift of doing cut-ins in the morning. "I was devastated," she said. "I knew it was a horrible demotion." But she didn't give up. She persisted and eventually landed the last thing a news anchor wanted, a job co-hosting a new local daytime talk show the station was developing. After the show became a modest hit, she was noticed by another local station, this one in Chicago. Despite the odds, her little show started beating talk-show king Phil Donahue, before it exploded into national syndication with a new name: *The Oprah Winfrey Show.*

"I don't want anyone who doesn't want me."

—Oprah Winfrey

Before bringing his characters to life in the blockbuster *Night Before Christmas,* Disney rejected Tim Burton. His work was deemed "too derivative of the Seuss works to be marketable." Yet this rejection didn't stop him. After graduating, he contacted Disney again and worked as an apprentice animator in 1980 before going on to set up and direct *Edward Scissorhands, Batman,* and even start up his own studio!

"Every story has a beginning, a middle, and an end. Not necessarily in that order."
—Tim Burton

Before she punched out some of the most famous words in culinary history on an old typewriter, *"For the Servantless American Cook,"* Julia Child was criticized for wanting to get a diploma by the headmistress of Le Cordon Bleu school in Paris, France. But that didn't stop her. Neither did getting her legendary manuscript, *Mastering the Art of French Cooking*, rejected repeatedly for the next decade. Instead, Julia kept on going until her epic 726-page book found a home with publisher Knopf, *ten years* later.

"The only real stumbling block is fear of failure. In cooking you've got to have a what-the-hell attitude."
—Julia Child

I thank God Craig rejected me in the cruelest of places in the world—middle school—as nothing would ever be as bad as that. Plus, Craig unintentionally gave me the courage to grow as a person, which prepared me to meet the love of my life, Bruce, a man who makes me feel like my heels never touch the ground!

"A lot of people ask me, 'How did you have the courage to walk up to record labels when you were 12 or 13 and jump right into the music industry?' It's because I knew I could never feel the kind of rejection that I felt in middle school. Because in the

music industry, if they're gonna say no to you, at least they're gonna be polite about it."

—Taylor Swift

Why Do You Doubt Yourself?

When you doubt yourself, you are throwing away your shot. You are the key to your success, and when your fears and doubts toss that key away, you are giving away your only chance of unlocking the door and succeeding. Why do we do this? The answer is easy—because somebody taught you to. And this is why you need to get away from these people in your life. They have done enough damage already, so get rid of them. Instead, surround yourself with positive folks who are cheering for you. Find yourself new friends and mentors, people who want to see you beam with certainty, rather than be riddled with doubt.

> *"Show me a successful individual and I'll show you someone who had real positive influences in his or her life. I don't care what you do for a living—if you do it well, I'm sure there was someone cheering you on or showing the way. A mentor."*
>
> —Denzel Washington

Learn to trust your own abilities and judgment. Even with great friends and mentors, it is essential that you can turn to yourself to erase the negative voices that come from deep within, the dark thoughts that you have been carefully taught over the years that have been internalized and believed. The good news is, if you can be taught to doubt yourself, you can also be untaught and then retaught to believe in yourself. Root out silence and replace fear with confidence because having questions is healthy, but letting them stop you from achieving your dreams is not. Doubt is a nasty habit that must be mastered if you want to be successful.

> *"I've learned that the mastery of self-doubt is the key to success."*
>
> —Will Smith

. . . .

Rob Shuter, thank you for the life-changing 4WORDANSWER! You have opened my eyes, and now I can't believe that I doubted myself for almost 40 years. I don't blame my parents; it was what they were taught from their parents and so on and so on. But that stops right now. I am going to teach my kids that anything is possible if they keep trying. I want them to know how **important** *both of them are. —Robin*

. . . .

You start to learn doubt at a very early age, from a parent or teacher or friends. It sinks its claws into you so deeply that it is difficult to remember a time when it wasn't there. It becomes so familiar that you might not even notice it inside you anymore, making it almost impossible to escape. Once it has invaded our minds, we seek it out for comfort as we get older, from partners and colleagues and the same people who infected us in the first place. We unknowingly surround ourselves with people who confirm the ugly lies we have internalized—that we are not good enough, that we don't deserve a good life, and that we are not

important—until our confidence is destroyed. Before long, the method of infection transforms from someone sabotaging you to you sabotaging yourself. It is very easy to develop self-destructive patterns of behavior when we think this is what we deserve. But it can be stopped. It can be reversed. The first step to doing so is finding enough confidence to learn to love yourself and believe that you are **important**! Stop sawing off the branch of the tree on which you are sitting. Don't hang yourself with the more-than-enough rope that you are given. Instead, love yourself. Build a swing with that rope and hang it from the highest branch of the tree where you once sat watching everything spring up and grow.

> *"I had to grow to love my body. I did not have a good self-image at first. Finally, it occurred to me, I'm either going to love me or hate me. And I chose to love myself. Then everything kind of sprung from there. Things that I thought weren't attractive became sexy. Confidence makes you sexy."*
>
> —Queen Latifah

The next time you hear that amazingly persuasive voice of self-doubt in your head or from others, don't get scared, get determined. Resolve to not listen to it anymore and to not let it hold you back from seizing opportunities that come your way. Grab every chance that comes your way. Disrupt those ugly thoughts right away by reminding yourself how many times in the past you have been frightened even though nothing bad ended up happening! The monster inside your head is far fiercer than anything you will meet in real life. I know, because I've spent time working for Barbara Walters! Wink.

"The enemy is fear. We think it is hate, but it is fear."
—Gandhi

Stop comparing yourself to others, especially others on social media. The only person you need to compare yourself to is yourself. Remember the positive things, not the negative, and think about your successes, not your failures. Focus on how far you have come and all the obstacles you have already triumphed over to get where you are right now. When fear pops back up, alleviate it by logically laying out what is troubling you. I've always been a big fan of a pros and cons list, finding it extremely helpful when I'm organizing my thoughts. Strive to be level-headed, rather than emotional, especially when thinking about yourself.

"To handle yourself, use your head; to handle others, use your heart."
—Eleanor Roosevelt

Thanks, Rob. I have the four words printed out in huge letters hanging in my office for everyone to see. We are much more positive and have stopped worrying about what our competition is doing and instead are just focusing on what we are doing. This has started to change all our lives in such a positive way, and our business—we are up 24%!" —Trent

What has helped me immeasurably with my own self-doubt is remembering that nobody really cares that much about what you say and do. This might seem a rather strange revelation to make in a chapter focusing on the fact we are all **important**; however, it is much easier to stop worrying about what other people might say or think when you realize that they don't say or think very much about you at all! Your name might pop up in the odd conversation amongst friends over drinks, the few days each year that Meghan Markle isn't dominating the headlines, but that's about it! This doesn't mean that you are not **important**. It means you are not as **important** to everyone else as you are to yourself, which is exactly as it should be. Have a little humility knowing people are way too busy thinking about their own lives to be thinking about yours. Some people don't even see what is in front of their very own noses. They're like the bunch of American tourists who stumbled upon an older lady and a younger male friend walking by Balmoral Castle. A member of the group asked the lady if she lived in the area. She humbly responded with a yes, in her English accent, adding that she had a house nearby. Then one of the Americans asked if she had ever met the queen! She responded "no," before pointing to her young friend and saying, "but he has." The tourists had no idea they were talking to Queen Elizabeth and her protection officer, Richard Griffin, who would later share the amazing story.

> *"Humility is not thinking less of yourself; it's thinking of yourself less."*
>
> —C. S. Lewis

Along with the Sarah Palin autobiography that I mentioned earlier, I have a copy of Greg Behrendt and Liz Tuccillo's brilliant, *He's Just Not That Into You* on my desk. It is a wonderful book, with an even better title because it explains in just six (not four) words that it's about them, not you. Knowing you are not the center of everyone's life removes an enormous amount of pressure and anxiety. The next time a coworker is snippy or a first date doesn't call back for a second, know that it has almost nothing to do with you. See the setback for what it is (temporary and something that happens to every one of us) and move on.

> *"Be who you are and say how you feel, because those who mind don't matter, and those who matter don't mind."*
> —Dr. Seuss

Finally, the best way to eliminate self-doubt is to be prepared. It is so much easier to be fearless when you know what you are doing. When you have the answers to all the questions, there is nothing to fear. I have been doing my show and reporting on celebrities for years, yet I still insist each morning before we tape that the team does a full run-through of the show to make sure we have the answer to every question that could possibly be asked. Madonna still rehearses her act forty years into her career. If she can, then so can you. You would be surprised how many superstars I've witnessed standing in front of a mirror at home before a big event, practicing. Everyone needs to do the work, and you are no exception. Before a big presentation in the office, a meeting, or even a first date, sharpen up your skills. Take your time to go over what you are about to do, read the research, be prepared, arrive early to be your best, and remember that you are **important**!

> *"By failing to prepare, you are preparing to fail."*
> —Benjamin Franklin

Instead of Asking "What's Wrong?" Ask This!

How many times have you asked, "What is wrong with me?" And how many times has that helped? Yet we keep doing it, asking over and over again the most unhelpful question that never yields any results. It has become almost automatic to ask, "What's wrong?" whenever we see someone who makes us uncomfortable. But this old default setting not only doesn't help, it prevents us from asking the new, real question: "What happened?"

> *"The secret of change is to focus all your energy not on fighting the old but on building the new."*
>
> —Socrates

Words are **important** and have such a huge impact that they shine with relevance. This is why we should not be connecting the feeling of being uncomfortable or sad with the word "wrong." There is nothing, and never has been anything, wrong with the way you feel. When bad things happen, feeling sad is absolutely right, appropriate, and totally normal. The next time you find yourself upset, or want to help a friend out in pain, stop asking, "What is wrong?" and start asking, "What happened?"

> *"I know nothing in the world that has as much power as a word. Sometimes I write one, and I look at it until it begins to shine."*
>
> —Emily Dickinson

> *Asking what happened instead of what's wrong is a game-changer. Before, when I couldn't talk to my boss about the raise that I deserve, I would ask, 'What's wrong with me?' which didn't help at all. Now I ask, 'What happened?' and it totally prepared me to move forward in the right way. There is nothing wrong with me, and I got the raise! —Jo*

If you want to be honest with yourself and be comfortable in your own skin, if you want to open up and tell your story, stop putting up walls. This is exactly what you are doing when you ask, "What is wrong?" No wonder the answer is always "nothing" when this question is asked! It is amazing to see the difference you will get by simply rephrasing a question. You cannot determine other people's responses, but you can choose and adjust your approach.

> *"I can't change the direction of the wind, but I can adjust my sails to always reach my destination."*
> —Jimmy Dean

We all have a unique story to tell—the good, the bad, and everything in-between that got us to where we are today. The key to understanding who you are right now is acknowledging what happened before. Finding peace in the present means you have to look to the past and understand what happened. Uncovering aspects of your life that are emotional red flags and triggers isn't easy and is inherently different for every one of us, but it's work that has to be done. For some, it is painful past relationships; for others, it's money issues. In reality, it can come from almost anything in your past that was never resolved. Identify your triggers to help you minimize exposure and navigate your way through future tricky situations. Learning to limit your exposure to painful situations is not running away from them or trying to create a bubble that cuts you off from the real world. Rather, being aware allows you to take action and take back your power. It is very difficult to manage and process emotions when we are triggered, which is why we end up simply reacting to them. These emotional scars we all have will take a very long time to heal and may never totally disappear. This is why we all need a strategy because ignoring the scars doesn't make them go away. Do the work, be patient, and know that there is nothing, and never was anything, wrong with you!

> *"We delight in the beauty of the butterfly, but rarely admit the changes it has gone through to achieve that beauty."*
>
> —Maya Angelou

People who see me on TV, listen to my podcast, or have drinks with me at Bottino in Chelsea find it hard to believe that I was once scared to speak up. As a young child with a lisp and a huge gap between my two front teeth that would whistle whenever I said a word beginning with "S," I would watch people enter the room and pray they wouldn't notice me. "Please don't speak to me. Please don't see me," I would repeat over and over inside my head. Even today, before I go live, some of those feelings come flooding back. But now, instead of asking, "What's wrong with me?" I ask, "What happened to me?" It changes everything. Everyone experiences a version of anxiety and depression in their lives due to myriad different reasons; however, once you confront your past, make peace with it, and choose to believe in yourself right now, you take the power out of the past and place it firmly into your hands in the present.

> *"Rejection triggers my anxiety and depression. Once I learn how to choose myself and be completely validated by that choice, I'll put the trigger in my hands and not in the hands of others."*
>
> —Lizzo

Thanks to *The 4 Word Answer*, I am now much kinder to that shy, scared little boy with the lisp who is still living inside me. Along with the help of a great dentist, Debra Glassman, and an exceptional speech therapist, that little guy will never be silenced again because there is not and never was anything wrong with him or you!

> *"There's nothing wrong with you. There's a lot wrong with the world you live in."*
>
> —Chris Colfe

It's Important to Do Something Just for You

When was the last time you did something just for you? Think about it. When was the last time you did one thing that wasn't about your job or kids or family or friends or partner? My guess is that you are having a harder time answering the question than you thought. That is because we all get so busy with our routines and lives that it seems there are not enough hours in the day to focus on ourselves anymore. But the truth is we are *not* too busy to do something for ourselves. Rather, we are making excuses because we don't believe that we are **important** enough to be a priority!

"No more excuses. I'm responsible for my mistakes and my choices."

—Brad Pitt

Busyness does not exist. You are never too busy to do something you really want to do. It is a defense mechanism that allows you to avoid doing the things that you find scary. It is an excuse that allows you to rationalize why you are putting off doing something out of your comfort zone. It shifts responsibility away from you and makes it so you don't have to deal with the real reason behind your lack of desire. By pretending you don't have enough time to do something, you don't have to confront your fears right now. But I guarantee that in the long run, it will mean you will have to deal with your regrets.

"We should all start to live before we get too old. Fear is stupid. So are regrets."

—Marilyn Monroe

I stopped making excuses and dealt with my biggest fear: being abandoned again. My mom left when I was a baby, and The 4 Word Answer made me finally deal with it. It is amazing how much my life has changed, including losing 80 lbs. that I put on to keep other people away. I am no longer too busy for me. I never really was, but I kept making excuses so I wouldn't have to deal with my past. This world needs more people like you, teaching them that they are never too busy to change. —Kelly

Age is one of the biggest excuses people tell themselves. Just like believing you are too busy, saying you are too old is not true. It wasn't until I was in my late forties that I started to chase my dreams, which, by then, felt like they had drifted away to a point where they were impossible to reach. Yet making excuses each day didn't bring them any closer! Author Suzanne Collins didn't write *The Hunger Games* until she was forty-six. Charles Darwin, who we all agree was pretty smart, was fifty when his *On the Origin of Species* changed the world. The Mona Lisa didn't flash us her mesmerizing smile until Leonardo Da Vinci was fifty-one. Hero on the Hudson, Chesley "Sully" Sullenberger III was fifty-seven years old when he landed US Airways Flight 1549 on the Hudson River and saved all 155 souls aboard. And Nelson Mandela didn't become president until he was in his seventies! So, think again the next time you think that your dreams have slipped away. You are not too old; you are too scared.

> *"It's never too late. Don't focus on what was taken away. Find something to replace it, and acknowledge the blessing you have."*
> —Drew Barrymore

Think about all the relationships in your life that won't develop, the passions that will never burn, and the desires that you are not making a priority. What are the wonderful things for which you are not making time? It took me almost five years to finish this book because I kept putting it off out of fear, which is nothing compared to how long it took me to build up my courage to learn to swim. I had used every excuse in the book to pretend to be too busy for over a decade. All that changed when I started to believe that I was **important** enough to do something for me.

It doesn't matter who you are or how busy you think your life might be—we can all find fifteen minutes each day for ourselves. The next time you are about to say, "I'm too busy" or "I'm too old" or any other excuse that you might use, be brutally honest with yourself and tell the truth—say, "It's just not a big enough priority!"

> *"One of the things I realized is that if you do not take control over your time and your life, other people will gobble it up. If you don't prioritize yourself, you constantly start falling lower and lower on your list."*
> —Michelle Obama

It's Important to Remember Why You Started

We all have days when we feel like quitting, when it gets too hard and the light at the end of the tunnel feels more like a train coming toward you! Those cold, rainy mornings when it's still dark out and you want nothing more than to stay home, safe under the covers in your warm bed. It is precisely on days like these, when you want to give in, that you need to remember why you started in the first place. Not every day can be a winning one, which is just fine, because it is on the days when you feel like you are losing that you are actually gaining the strength and determination you will need to win on other days.

> *"Strength does not come from winning. Your struggles develop your strengths. When you go through*

hardships and decide not to surrender, that is true strength."

—Arnold Schwarzenegger

The bigger the dream, the more time it takes to make it come true. Time gives you both the experience you will require to turn your dreams into reality and the tools you will need to handle both success and defeat. Success demands a lot of failure, testing you over and over again, to make sure that you deserve to win. Just like metal is stronger than ever once it's been forged in fire, you will be made just as tough by failure. Learn to never give up or in, and remember, you have only persevered enough when you have succeeded.

"Perseverance is failing 19 times and succeeding the 20th."

—Julie Andrews

I've been so busy lately that I forgot why I started. Not just at work, but also in my marriage. I was just doing things, my job, being a mom, being a wife—and I had forgotten the why! Now I have cut out all the noise and gone back to basics. How did I lose sight of why we got married and decided to have a family? It was because we love each other deeply, and because of you, we will never forget that again. —Jee

Success doesn't happen overnight, which is why you must constantly remind yourself why you started. Once you remember, the noise disappears. It will vanish along with the people telling you that you shouldn't, couldn't, and wouldn't. Leave them all behind, transforming their negative thoughts into their problems, not yours. The beginning of any success story is always more **important** than the end. Never forget the exciting thoughts you had when you started, the moments that were full of hope and joy and spent dreaming about what the future could be. These feelings are your armor, the magic cape you must not forget to put on to repel all the doubts and doubters. Let them waste as much of their time as they want judging what you do, as you spend each minute of your own time marching ahead toward your goals with your cape floating in the wind. Don't let anyone distract you from your goals; instead, remain focused on knowing exactly who you are and why you started.

> *"The difference between winners and losers is winners know exactly who they are and aren't scared to be authentic." "I am who I am and I know who I am."*
> —Wendy Williams

Beware! It's not just other people's thoughts that will try to hold you back. The most dangerous opinions often come from inside your own head. As the long journey drags on, doubt creeps in, and voices will start to ask, "What if it doesn't work out? What if people laugh? What if it is just too hard?" These wicked whispers will try to stop you dead in your tracks, which is why you need a solid foundation. The reason you started, the beginning on which you are building the dream, is the foundation that must be solid and strong enough to survive all the doubts and hold you steady as you build all the way up to the stars!

"Every great dream begins with a dreamer. Always remember, you have within you the strength, the patience, and the passion to reach for the stars to change the world."

— Harriet Tubman

"I had been holding myself back and didn't even realize it until discovering The 4 Word Answer. Now, I've gone from part-time to full-time and from doing "just fine" to doing JUST GREAT! Get out of your own way and dump those people in your life who don't believe in you. I am **important** enough to be better than just OK!" —Greg

---

The reason I started changing my life was that I had no other choice. Everything was going wrong, and I needed to stop and start again. The only thing I knew how to do was be a publicist and a reporter—so, that's what I did. I opened up my computer and started to report. I researched, wrote down, and reported everything I knew about A-list celebrity lives and what made these extraordinary people so successful. I hoped that what I discovered could help at least one other person, but helping others was not the reason why I started. I started because the one person I needed to help was myself. I couldn't stop thinking about my experiences. What if I was right? What if I could do this? What if I was smart enough? What if I was kind enough? What if I was **important** enough to find the answer? The truth is, I started because the answer to all these questions was yes! And that "yes" would stop my pain. I didn't have to quit on myself or live another minute being so unkind to myself and others. I

ROB SHUTER

didn't have to be sick and tired of feeling stupid anymore, making bad decision after bad decision, and I didn't have to feel so very unimportant for one more minute, hour, day, or year. This is the reason I started. What's yours?

> *"Pain is temporary. It may last a minute, or an hour, or a day, or a year, but eventually it will subside and something else will take its place. If I quit, however, it lasts forever. That surrender, even the smallest act of giving up, stays with me. So, when I feel like quitting, I ask myself, which would I rather live with?"*
> —Lance Armstrong

If You Are Not Doing the Work, You Don't Deserve the Results

The key to success is putting in the work. Big dreams only come true if you work toward them every single day. No one can do it for you. Not your parents, your friends, your partner, or anyone else. Only you can do the work that will let you succeed, which is why it is impossible to bribe or buy your way there; the people who cheat always get found out! Effort is the only currency that success accepts, and the more you are willing to spend, the more you will receive!

> *"We are responsible for our own fate, we reap what we sow, we get what we give, we pull in what we put out. I know these things for sure."*
> —Madonna

THE 4 WORD ANSWER

I thought I could fake my way to the top. I've always cheated at tests and diets and even life…but it has never ended well. If I spent as much time doing the work as I did playing the system, I would be at the very top right now! Now, I don't cheat anymore. My rich parents or friends can't do it for me. I am doing it myself, and for the first time in my life, it feels AMAZING! To focus every day and learn something new is so much better than cheating. We are all responsible for our own lives; why wouldn't you want to work hard at that? I always felt like a phony until you, Rob. Now I'm the real deal—just like you, my friend! ROB SHUTER'S 4 WORD ANSWER kicks ass. —Blake

Success is not an accident; success is for people who do the work. If you really put in the work, you will get the most amazing results out of life. If you sort of try, you will sort of succeed. If you try once and then give up, you will get nowhere and have no chance of success. You have to listen. You have to read. You have to watch and learn your craft. The person who succeeds is the person who shows up one more time than the person who quits. If you choose to wait until you think you are ready, you'll be waiting for the rest of your life. Show up, keep going, and eventually, you will get what you deserve. Stop saying you'll do it tomorrow, get out of your head, and keep going because you have been hitting the snooze button on your dreams for far too long already.

> *"I think people sometimes don't pay enough attention to what they do. I've done well, but the*

reason is pretty simple: I've worked my ass off. The toughest thing a performer can do is make it look as if it comes off easy."

—Justin Timberlake

Clean out your negative thoughts and replace them with ones that let you get the work done. Did you really have a bad day or was it just a bad four minutes that you spent the rest of the day obsessing about? Don't let a rude email from your boss, the wrong coffee from the barista, the passive-aggressive Facebook post from a stranger, or the self-absorbed call from a family member ruin the rest of your day. A bad four minutes is just a bad four minutes. It doesn't have to stop you from doing the work unless you let it. Instead of thinking you "have to," start thinking that you "get to." The first few years I got to be on TV, I was so excited, thrilled to be talking to Kathie Lee and Hoda Kotb, whom I had spent years watching from the comfort of my sofa; however, after a while, the excitement rubbed off. It went from being a little fun to also being a little bit of work. Having to stay in the night before to learn my script while everyone else was out partying and having to get up early in the morning to get to the studio to have my hair pulled and face painted got old surprisingly fast. Until I checked myself. "Who gets to be on America's number one morning show?" I asked myself with a cold hard slap across the face—that I needed! I switched up my thoughts immediately, realizing that sacrificing one night out and an extra hour of sleep wasn't a burden. It was a dream come true.

"Dreams do come true, if only we wish hard enough. You can have anything in life if you will sacrifice everything else for it."

—J.M. Barrie from *Peter Pan*

Tonight, I had a chance to give someone my number, and I did! At first, I hesitated because I didn't want to get hurt or rejected. I told myself—you 'don't have to give him your number'; rather, 'you get to give this amazing guy your number!' He called me the next day! LIFE IS GREAT! —Anne

Diddy would laugh when the media called him an overnight success, knowing that he worked for years huffing and puffing (which legend has it is how he got this name), producing weekly dance parties. Long before his face was all over the magazines and newspapers, Puff was hustling at his internship at Uptown Records, learning the business from the inside out. Puff, and everyone else who has been discovered as an "overnight success," knows it all starts with hard work—years and years of doing the work.

"There's no such thing as overnight success. That's my concern with a show like American Idol. It encourages the false belief that there's a kind of magic, that you can be 'discovered.' That may be the way television works, but it's not the way the world works. Rising to the top of any field requires an enormous amount of dedication, focus, drive,

talent, and 99 factors that they don't show on television. It's not simply about being picked. Which, by the way, is why very few of the anointed winners on American Idol have gone on to true success. Most have flamed out and gone away. That should tell us something."

—Malcolm Gladwell

If you do the work, you deserve the results. Ask yourself, if you knew it was going to take years to get where you want to be, would you still want it? That is exactly what it's going to take. It all starts with you saying out loud, "Yes, I am **important**!" When you have the courage to believe it, really believe it, you might be destined to change far more than just your own future…you might change the world, too.

*"You may not always have a comfortable life and you will not always be able to solve all of the world's problems at once, but don't ever underestimate the **importance** you can have because history has shown us that courage can be contagious and hope can take on a life of its own."*

—Michelle Obama

C
H
A
P
T
E
R

You Is...(insert your name)!

I WAS IN AWE OF JENNIFER LOPEZ EVEN LONG BEFORE I started working for her. This was not only because of her talents, as she would admit that there are much better singers, actresses, and even dancers than her, but because she had star quality! There was something about Jennifer that made every room she entered dazzle. It felt like the lights shone brighter when Jen was around. And at the center of all this magical energy, the electricity that turned on the lights was the fact that Jennifer was totally comfortable being herself.

> *"You've got to love yourself first. You've got to be OK on your own before you can be OK with somebody else. You've got to value yourself and know that you're worth everything!"*
>
> —Jennifer Lopez

Jennifer's power doesn't come from the fact that she gets to look in the mirror every day and say, "You are...Jennifer Lopez." No, her power comes from the fact that she knows exactly who Jennifer Lopez is! She has discovered, accepted, and learned to love herself, even her flaws (yes, the great Jennifer Lopez does have a few)! I know it's easy to look at someone like Jennifer and say, "I would accept myself, too, if I were rich, powerful, and beautiful," but that is missing the point. Jennifer is only rich, powerful, and looks as polished as she does because she knows who she is and accepts it. Acceptance made Jennifer a superstar, not the other way around, because success isn't about money, looks, or ability! Success is about knowing yourself, really knowing who you are, and believing in it.

> "It just takes faith and belief in yourself, and you've got to dig deep into that. That has to come from you—nobody's going to give you that. You can have a great mentor, a great partner, a great love in your life who gives you confidence and makes you feel great about yourself. And that's all wonderful, but at the end of the day, if you don't believe it, all of that means nothing."
>
> —Jennifer Lopez

Get to know every single detail about who you are, no matter how small or how big. Accept the good, the bad, the beautiful, and even the ugly! Remember that none of us is perfect. That's what makes us human. When we learn to recognize and accept ourselves, that's what makes us happy, successful, and able to discover our best.

"I'm not here to be perfect and I'm not here to be anything but my best, whatever that means for me."
—Jennifer Lopez

Getting to Know You, Getting to Know All about You

What makes you, you? It seems like an easy question, yet it is impossible to answer if you don't truly know yourself. Tune out the rest of the world and build an unbreakable connection with the most important thing in your life—you! Suddenly, the question becomes much easier to answer. "Getting to Know You," the song Anna sang in *The King and I* to the children of the King of Siam, is the song we all need to start singing to ourselves. Get to know all about yourself, and not just the small stuff like your favorite color or your favorite flavor of ice cream, but also the big stuff, the stuff that makes you uniquely you. Until you know who you are, nothing else will make sense.

"Knowing yourself is the beginning of all wisdom."
—Aristotle

Getting to know yourself is an unpredictable process of discovery that will make your mind expand. Coming face-to-face with your better angels and your worst demons is complicated, but it will provide answers to all your questions for the rest of your life. Remember that every one of us is born a stranger. The process of getting to know yourself and getting comfortable in your own skin is not automatic. Unlike growing taller or older, it doesn't happen on its own. There is nothing natural or organic about discovering who you are; rather, it is something you have to consciously choose to do. Otherwise, it is perfectly possible to live your entire life without getting to know the real you. Discovering who you are takes courage, purpose, and time. Accepting who that person turns out to be takes even longer.

> *"Being comfortable in your own skin is one of the most important things to achieve. I'm still working on it!"*
>
> —Kate Mara

You've helped change my life, and we've never even met! However, I feel like I know you, which was more than I could say about myself. I didn't have a clue who I was before the 4WA. I'm forty years old and might as well have been living with a stranger. I didn't even know what my favorite color was. It wasn't easy getting to know myself, but it is certainly worth it because I just found out that I am awesome. For the first time ever, I feel comfortable in my own skin, thanks to you! —Rachel

Sooner or later, not knowing who you are becomes painfully obvious to everyone, including you. The quiet frustration of living with a stranger you are not comfortable with becomes louder and louder as you grow older. It gets increasingly difficult not knowing the person that you can't get away from the more years you spend together. Still, a shockingly large number of people try to run away from themselves by trying to live in denial or numb the pain, rather than starting the long process of discovering who they are.

> *"I was once afraid of people saying, 'Who does she think she is?' Now I have the courage to stand and say 'This is who I am.'"*
>
> —Oprah Winfrey

Knowing yourself means being aware of what you like and what you don't like. What matters to you and what doesn't. What your strengths are and what weaknesses you bring to the table. What you admire and what you don't. It means understanding your tolerances and limitations. Identifying what drives your desires and dreams and what turns you off. This is a lot to know. But knowing what makes you unique and different from everyone else also gives you power.

> *"Being unique and different was a really good thing. When I walked into my agent's office for the first time, they looked at me and said, 'Wow, we have nobody on our books like you.' And they signed me on my second day here."*
>
> —Rebel Wilson

Knowing and respecting who you are will change your life, leading you to a place where your outside actions and inner feelings align. The smallest decisions you make all day (like what you are going to eat) and the big choices (like who you are going to spend your life with) will all be much easier. When you become your own best friend, you become your own best advocate, able to focus on saying yes to what is right for you and no to what isn't.

> *"You have a right to say no. Most of us have very weak and flaccid 'no' muscles. We feel guilty for saying no. We get ostracized and challenged for saying no, so we forget it's our choice. Your 'no' muscle has to be built up to get to a place where you can say, 'I don't care if that's what you want. I don't want that. No.'"*
> —Iyanla Vanzant

Living a lie is not an act you can keep up for very long. Sooner or later, the truth will always come out. I know because I spent over a decade trying to fool myself and everyone else that I was someone I was not. Today, I don't recognize that scared guy who once told so many lies that he couldn't keep them straight. It's ironic because a lot of them were to cover up the fact that I am not straight! Living a lie is like being under a wicked spell that can only be broken by finding my true love's kiss—which I found not in the form of my Prince Charming, Bruce, but rather from me! We all have to learn to love ourselves to break the ugly spell. That is only possible after we take the time to get to know and become best friends with that scared kid inside all of us!

> *"Being honest may not get you a lot of friends, but it'll always get you the right ones."*
> —John Lennon

> *I made a choice to stop living a lie, and my world changed for the better forever. Instead of waiting for a prince or knight in shining armor to come along, I made myself the hero of my story. That scared little girl is never far away, but now that I have been introduced to her, I can be kind and let her know that she is important and smart. Rob, you are the fairy godmother we all deserve to have! Cheers! —Pam*

I am lucky that my coming-out story involves a lot of love and acceptance. But being honest with myself did not go over well with everyone in my working-class town. There were certainly friends who walked away, and my own sister even threatened to out me. It's not just gay people who carry secrets, however. Each and every one of us is hiding something in some closet somewhere, which is why we all need to swing open those closed doors and come out and say, "This is me!" as frightening as this may be.

I know it isn't easy putting your own needs above everyone else's. Growing up, I can't think of a single time when anyone encouraged me to think about myself before thinking of others. Putting others first is celebrated as the marker of being a "good person." What if everything we have been taught is backwards, though? What if safe, happy, and healthy starts with you?

> *"Never make someone a priority when all you are to them is an option."*
>
> —Maya Angelou

It wasn't until I started to focus on me and on getting to know myself that the bitterness disappeared. It took me a long time to let go of what I had been taught and carried around since I was a child. The joy I felt when I finally understood that looking out for myself was not selfish (in fact, it was the opposite) was memorable. Until you take care of yourself, you are incapable of taking care of anyone else. Remember that the opposite of self-love is self-hatred, and if my great love of international travel has taught me anything, it is to always put your mask on first before helping others.

> *"To love oneself is the beginning of a life-long romance."*
>
> —Oscar Wilde

Get to Know Your Likes and Dislikes

The first time I asked myself, "What do you like and what do you dislike?" I didn't know the answer. I didn't know what I liked and, just as importantly, what I disliked because I didn't know myself very well at all. The reason lots of people find this question difficult is that it takes a lot of confidence to be yourself in a world that is constantly judging—a confidence that shines so brightly, it shows off every color in your rainbow without apology!

> *"Do not allow people to dim your shine because they are blinded. Tell them to put on some sunglasses, 'cause we were born this way!"*
>
> —Lady Gaga

Knowing what you like and what you don't like is not the same as knowing what is popular and what is unpopular. How many times have you been in a restaurant and overheard someone ask the waiter, "What's your most popular dish?" Clearly, that person doesn't know or trust themselves very much! Do you have friends who only support the most popular sports teams or performers? Maybe that person trying to be like everyone else is you! On the flip side, it is way too easy to parrot other people's dislikes and trash what isn't popular. I admit that standing up for my love of *The Sound of Music* never won me any cool points. Making fun of a nun singing on the top of a mountain in Austria is admittedly shooting fish in a barrel! That is why it takes the very confidence that Maria Von Trapp sang about to be whoever you want to be. Always express your inner "do-re-mi" and never allow the popular choice to dictate your likes and dislikes.

> *"It's not easy being a Barry Manilow fan. You get a lot of [crap] for that. It's easier for people to say that they like Bruce Springsteen or Bon Jovi than it is for them to say they like what I do, because what I do is so personal. It's like talking about religion—you just don't talk about it. The kind of music that I make is yours, it's your personal thing. You take it to your room and listen to it by yourself. You don't talk about it. It's easy to say you love Steely Dan, but it's not so easy to say that you love an artist whose music has helped you through some very lonely times. I may be one of the guys who does that."*
>
> —Barry Manilow

> *Rob, I got up yesterday after I put The 4 Word Answer into effect... I am kind, I am smart, I am important, and I am CLARE! Plus, I am the world's biggest Barry Manilow fan, and I am proud to shout it from the roof-tops, thanks to you. You won't remember me, but we met at Barry's show, and you told me to not listen to anyone other than myself. Which I am now doing every day, thanks to you, and BARRY! —Clare*

Don't rush into deciding what you believe. These are things you must decide for yourself, and you can take as much time as you want. Growing up, my friends loved playing sports on the weekend and couldn't understand anyone who didn't. Kicking a football—or worse, running around in circles with a bat—was their idea of fun, never mine! Likewise, as I grew older, there were things I wanted to love so much but didn't. I tried to like opera more times than I can remember. I wanted nothing more than to enjoy reading a big fat classic book for hours! Alas, knowing my Verdi from my Puccini or my Dickens from my Brontë was just not for me.

> *"If we stop defining each other by what we are not and start defining ourselves by what we are, we can all be freer."*
>
> —Emma Watson

Never give up part of yourself just to fit in. Always be true to your likes and dislikes and remember that nobody has to like or dislike them except you! Learn to speak up and say no instead of yes to situations you don't enjoy. When you stop trying to be someone you are not, it gives you more time to be who you are.

> *"It took me years to internalize that someone could look at me and tell that I am transgender. That is not only OK, that is beautiful. Trans is beautiful. All the things that make me uniquely and beautifully trans, my big hands, my big feet, my wide shoulders, my deep voice, are beautiful."*
>
> —Laverne Cox

A huge part of knowing who you are is knowing what makes you feel good and what makes you feel bad. It is as unique for each of us as our fingerprints. This is why we all must experiment with a sense of wonder, trying out lots of new and different things that might enrich our lives, before we can say what we like and what we don't! For years, I always assumed I hated sushi—probably because of my love for the fish swimming around in the many tanks in my apartment—until I went to the fancy restaurant Nobu and reluctantly tasted their yellowtail and jalapeño dish. Let's just say, are those chopsticks or are you happy to sashimi? Trying different cuisines is just the tip of the getting-to-know-you iceberg. There is so much more to experience that lies beneath! Think about every single aspect of your life and audit it into what you like and don't like columns. The goal is to end up with a life where your "like" column is full and the "don't like" column is empty.

"You will enrich your life immeasurably if you approach it with a sense of wonder and discovery, and always challenge yourself to try new things."
—Nate Berkus

One of the biggest time commitments in most people's lives is our jobs. That's why it is essential that we all do something that makes us happy. Another huge area of all our lives is our family and friends, so we also need to seek out people we enjoy spending time with and say goodbye to those we don't! From the minute you wake up to the moment you go to bed, make sure you like what you are doing. Take a deep dive into all the relationships in your life—dating, friendships, work, hobbies, and yes, even family—with an open mind because when you understand all of these interactions, you will discover the truth about the most important relationship you are ever going to have: the relationship with yourself.

"It's sad, but sometimes moving on with the rest of your life starts with goodbye."
—Carrie Underwood

ROB, I listen to your podcast, and I love when you talk about being happy. I was miserable in my high-powered job, so I went back to college to follow my dreams. I am now teaching, and I have never been happier. Leaving a job that pays well is scary, but you have to say goodbye to be able to say 'ELLO, 'ELLO, 'ELLO! Love you! —Romaine

Once you discover what you like and don't like, make a mental note. Write it down and be sure to look at it often. Make sure the first entry on your "like" list is you. It will act as your own personal North Star, guiding you home when you spiral off course and forget what you enjoy!

> *"The most important relationship in your life is the relationship you have with yourself. Because no matter what happens, you will always be with yourself."*
>
> —Diane Von Furstenberg

What Beliefs and Values Matter to You?

At first, the values and beliefs that we hold are not really ours. They have been thrust upon us by our parents, teachers, friends, and relatives in such an all-immersive way that it takes years before we even ask, "Do I actually believe all this stuff?" Some people just adopt them with no questions asked, taking on for a lifetime what others believe as their own. Don't be one of these people! Stop, ask, and learn to think for yourself. When you think for yourself, you don't need anyone else's opinion but your own.

> *"I've learned to trust myself, to listen to truth, to not be afraid of it, and to never try to hide it."*
>
> —Sarah McLachlan

Instead of trusting what has passively entered your life, actively choose what beliefs and values matter to you. Think about how you want to live your life, what is important to you, and what isn't. Focus on what you want your core values to be, the moral code and the principles that are non-negotiable. This is the key to the way your values and the way you live your life align. The better the fit, the better the life you will live. If they don't fit, you will know you need to make some serious adjustments because nothing will feel "right."

> *"Values are like fingerprints. Nobody's are the same,*
> *but you leave them all over everything you do."*
> —Elvis Presley

You can convince yourself that you are living life in accordance with your core values up to a certain point. At the end of the day, pretending that a few bad decisions do not change who you really are will not work. The fear of change is real, but so is the reality of living a lie. Something has to change before you can find peace and happiness. You can either change the way you live or change what you believe, but it has to be one.

> *"My decision to end my marriage was such a*
> *risk to lose ratings and lose my fan base. I had to*
> *take that risk for my inner peace and to be happy*
> *with myself."*
> —Kim Kardashian

As a young gay kid growing up in a homophobic world outside of Birmingham, England, I spent years trying to change who I was rather than changing what I believed. Life became more and more miserable for that confused young man trying so hard to be straight, pretending to like girls and praying he would meet the right one and live happily ever after. The soul-destroying lie got harder and harder as I grew older, watching friends experience young love, until one day, it was impossible to live the lie anymore. Knowing I had tried and failed to change myself, I had no choice but to change my beliefs and values. It was painful and scary throwing out everything I had ever been taught about love and marriage and Adam and Eve, but it was much easier than continuing living hating myself. In the end, my prayers were answered, and I did meet the right one and live happily ever after—except his name was Bruce!

> *"It took me a long time not to judge myself through someone else's eyes."*
>
> —Sally Field

The 4 Word Answer rules! Go listen to ROB SHUTER, and it will change your life. I had to change my life or my beliefs when my son recently told me he was gay. My life was anchored around my children and the church, a very conservative church that I had been going to for years. Despite what I pretended, gay people or anyone different wasn't welcomed. In fact, they were pushed away. My son is the most important person in my life and losing him was not an option. I have found a new place to worship, knowing my god recognizes all love. God bless you, Rob Shuter. —Anonymous

Beliefs and values are only important when they are yours. It is your life, and only you can decide what matters to you. Find the combination that is tailor-made for you. Honesty, integrity, security, flexibility, wisdom, financial comfort, loyalty, excellence, responsibility, or ambition only matter if you believe and value them. Getting to know yourself means finding out the exact ingredients to make your life delicious!

> *"True beauty is not related to what color your hair is or what color your eyes are. True beauty is about who you are as a human being, your principles, your moral compass."*
>
> —Ellen DeGeneres

What Are You Good at and Bad At?

An essential part of getting to know yourself is getting to know what you are good at and what you are not so good at. Knowing what your strengths are allows you to focus on them and on success. For some, these talents are very obvious, flashing lights from the moment they are born, waiting to illuminate the rest of their life. For others, like my good self, it may take a little longer to discover them. They are hiding and need a little more coaxing out before they shine. Don't worry if they are not obvious. We all possess gifts. Some are natural, and some are learned with hard work and determination. If you haven't found yours yet, keep looking because I promise that there is something you are good at. The hard part is finding it. Don't be surprised if your strengths show up and reveal themselves in your weakest moments because these gifts, whatever they may be, are your superpowers, waiting until you really need them to appear. They give you confidence,

self-esteem, and a strong foundation on which you can build
happiness and success, so start looking.

> *"You're much stronger than you think you are.*
> *Trust me."*
>
> —Spider-Man

When most people think about "strengths," they focus on
physical abilities and skills; however, that definition is way too
limiting. Mental abilities such as character, loyalty, respect, and
fairness are also great strengths. I knew at an early age that I
would never be the star of any gym class. My balance was so bad
that I would often fall over when I tried to kick a ball; with one
arm much stronger than the other, I was literally left running
around in circles! However, I also discovered at an early age that
I possessed the gift of knowing everyone's business. When my
brother Douglas' marriage was secretly falling apart, I knew.
The time my sister Christine was dating a person of color, I was
cheering. And I knew the truth about Santa Claus long before
anyone else in my class. At the time, I didn't see my gift as a
skill and would have swapped it in a hot second to be great with
a bat and ball, but not anymore. Being good at listening made
other people feel comfortable telling me all their secrets. There's
irony for you, considering at the time I was hiding a big fat gay
secret myself! My empathy and outright nosiness have served
me very well throughout my life, even steering me toward my
gossip career.

> *"You have brains in your head. You have feet in*
> *your shoes. You can steer yourself in any direction*
> *you choose. You're on your own, and you know*

what you know. And you are the guy who'll decide where to go."

—Dr. Seuss

Just listened to your show…and my impulse was to connect with you right away, so that's what I am doing. All my life I have been fighting what I am good at and what I love to do. I love writing, but I ended up working in a bank for a lot of bad reasons. But after The 4 Word Answer, I submitted one of my short stories in a competition, and I WON!!! You have given me the confidence to try and turn my side hustle into a career. I have since gotten a freelance gig as a writer for an online site, and I have never been happier. I'm not a wealthy person, but now I am a happy person. —Annabelle

Knowing your weaknesses is just as important as knowing your strengths. Both give you the ability to make the right choices and decisions for you. That is not to say that you should stop doing things just because you are not great at them, but rather, enjoy them while knowing the truth. I play the trumpet very badly. It gives me far more joy than it gives my unfortunate audience! Knowing this, I am able to take pleasure from my musical hobby without expecting to make a living playing for the New York Philharmonic! The key to happiness and success is accepting the truth about yourself. Acknowledging that I am never going to be the next Chris Botti has left me with more time to be the best Rob Shuter!

"At Facebook, we try to be a strengths-based organization, which means we try to make jobs fit around people rather than make people fit around jobs. We focus on what people's natural strengths are and spend our management time trying to find ways for them to use those strengths every day."
—Sheryl Sandberg

Facing your weaknesses is frightening, but also very productive. In fact, looking into the eyes of what you find terrifying frees you to be able to move forward. Confronting your weaknesses is a liberating experience because when you point them out before others do, you take the power away. Learning to own what you are not good at is as important as ownership of what you do well, as both are parts of you.

"Be happy with being you. Love your flaws. Own your quirks. And know that you are just as perfect as anyone else, exactly as you are."
—Ariana Grande

Let me confess—my speelling (wink) and punctuation and grammar is terrible! Acknowledging a problem is the first step in finding a solution, which in my case was finding a brilliant copy editor, my cousin, Leney! Now, when someone makes fun of me for not knowing my yours and my your's, instead of getting defensive, I agree! There is nothing anyone can say that will hurt you anymore when you know the truth about yourself. Knowing exactly who you are removes all the fears of being exposed, found out, or discovered as a fraud and replaces those with peace, peace, and peace!

"I've made peace with the fact that the things that I thought were weaknesses or flaws were just me. I like them."

—Sandra Bullock

Take a long hard look at all your interests because they are a compass pointing you toward what you are good at. Think about your passions and hobbies that you love to do. What makes you happy? What are you curious about? We only have one life to live, so we might as well make the most of it by doing things we enjoy. I have never met anyone who is really good at something they hated. So, get swept up by your interests, hobbies, and things you love. Protect them with a vengeance and build a life around what you love. When you next meet someone, don't ask what they do for a living first; instead, ask them about what hobbies they have. When the conversation eventually turns to work, which it always does, you will find that the happiest people are always the ones who have the strongest connection between their interests and their jobs. Make sure you are one of these people, too.

"You can only become truly accomplished at something you love. Don't make money your goal. Instead, pursue the things you love doing and then do them so well that people can't take their eyes off of you."

—Maya Angelou

My relationship with myself has improved since I started enjoying my hobbies again. I had given up dancing and sports because I was too busy working and paying my bills. Then a work colleague asked me to join a swimming team. I LOVE IT. Being back in the water has given me life again, so much so that I applied for a coaching job that just opened up. I might not get it, but I know my future has to involve sports, and it will. THE 4 WORD ANSWER has become my mantra. YOU ARE ANDREA AND YOU LOVE SPORTS! Thanks Rob! —Andrea

Surround yourself with your hobbies or passions. No matter how successful or busy you get, never abandon or throw them away. Emma Watson will always be a busy actress after playing Hermione Granger in the *Harry Potter* series, but Emma always finds the time to take part in her Zen workouts. Jennifer Garner always manages to find a moment in her life to enjoy playing the saxophone. Susan Sarandon's hobby of playing ping-pong brings her so much joy that she opened up a ping-pong club in New York. And Taylor Swift will always have room amongst her many awards for a new handmade snow globe she created. The point is, even if you are selling out stadiums, never be too busy for your hobbies or passions. If you want to fill a Mason jar with glitter and water, don't let anyone stop you from doing just that.

"It can be coins or sports or politics or horses or music or faith… the saddest people I've ever met in life are the ones who don't care deeply about anything at all. Passion and satisfaction go hand

in hand, and without them, any happiness is only
temporary, because there's nothing to make it last."
—Nicholas Sparks

Find a way to follow your passions, and you will change your life. I have always loved music and theatre and the creative people it attracts, despite being a terrible actor, dancer, singer, and, yes, trumpet player! What did I do? I found a way to get involved without having to say a single line, dance a single step, or sing a single note. I got a job selling ice creams at the Edinburgh Playhouse in Scotland! It might not seem the obvious way to get involved with something I loved, but it was the only job that was open that I could sort of do. I wanted to be part of this world so much that I found a way to get in selling ice creams during the intermission of *Phantom*, *Les Misérables*, and the brand-new musical called *Barry Manilow's Copacabana* before it headed to London's West End. It was also the first time I met my sexy husband, Bruce Sussman—I literally sold him what has turned out to be the most expensive ice cream of his entire life! I didn't make a lot of money wearing that red bolero jacket with gold trim and selling chocolate or vanilla cornets, but it started me off on a lifetime full of meeting the most extraordinary, talented, and creative people I could ever hope to call friends. All because I found a way to get myself in!

"I say always follow your passion, no matter what,
because even if it's not the same financial success,
it'll lead you to the money that'll make you the
happiest."
—Ellen DeGeneres

Dear Rob, I'm writing to say thank you. I took a receptionist job just to get into the TV business. It did exactly what you said it would do and got me into the world of television. I have met the most amazing people, and now, I'm an assistant producer, all because I took a job that was open to get me in the door. Thank you! —Mark

The place in this world where we will be happy and successful is different for every single one of us. But how we find it is exactly the same for all of us. Take what you are good at very seriously. Success doesn't come from your job or how much money you earn. Success only comes from people, especially from you. Get away from the places and people where you struggle and have no passion; find the environment that you care about and want to preserve as you learn your craft—even if it means starting out selling ice creams!

> *"If you want to be successful in a particular field of endeavor, I think perseverance is one of the key qualities. It's very important that you find something that you care about, that you have a deep passion for, because you're going to have to devote a lot of your life to it."*
>
> —George Lucas

What Do You Admire in Others?

The way we see other people tells us a lot about ourselves. Do you ever compare yourself to others? Get jealous and insecure when you see what an amazing life people you follow on Instagram seem to live or wonder how that coworker always seems to be on vacation? It is way too easy to get sucked into other people's lives, wondering how they got that cute date, what secret product they are using on their hair, or why they seem to have no trouble at all keeping off the weight! I know I have been guilty of all the above. It wasn't until I got to know myself that I found out why I felt so envious.

> *"You can only be jealous of someone who has something you think you ought to have yourself."*
> —Margaret Atwood

Once you get to know yourself, you see other people in a different way. Instead of being jealous, you will see admiration. Instead of being envious, you will be inspired. And rather than being resentful, you will discover goals. I used to get insanely jealous of the lives of many rich people, but no one more than the talented Barry Manilow. Of all the people I know very well, Barry has the most. Sitting in his airline terminal-sized Palm Springs house and listening to the songs that make the whole world sing, I could not believe the lap of luxury a human being and his lucky dogs called home.

I was resentful of the life Barry got to live, with his gardeners, assistant, driver, fans, and even a florist who arrived with magnificent arrangements. As someone who loves flowers, this one really drove me crazy! It wasn't until I got to know myself very well that all these feelings disappeared. It turns out the Rob I got to know didn't really want Barry's life at all. I love my privacy way too much to ever want to be any more well-known than I am. Heaven for me is getting a good night's sleep every evening in my own bed next to the man I love, rather than being alone in a hotel in Las Vegas. To be honest, I'm the type of person who has never really enjoyed a birthday party of more than four people applauding when I blow out my candles! I like the way I'm growing old and I love disappearing into a corner of Bottino's with Bruce and friends, not worrying about what's going to show up in the newspapers. The truth is I have created the life that is right for me, and it turns out that for just twenty dollars a bunch, I can buy the most amazing fresh flowers each week from my local bodega on 23rd Street and Ninth Avenue. Simply put, I admire Barry, but the price it costs to be him is way too high for me.

> *"Transform jealousy to admiration, and what you admire will become part of your life."*
>
> —Yoko Ono

Listened to your show. I've come to realize how big my inner jealous voice has been. Not only has it had a huge impact on my self-confidence, but it has also crippled my ability to move forward with my own life because I am too busy obsessing about others. Now when I feel jealous, I stop and look to see what I admire about that person. It has been a game-changer. Instead of wasting time hating others, I'm focusing on what they are doing that I want to be part of my life. Instead of hating Kate's amazing body, I joined the gym! BOOM... Thank you! Tina

When I was a publicist, I would make sure that I knew who made each and every one of my clients jealous. Jessica Simpson and Britney Spears. Jon Bon Jovi and the other Jersey rocker, Bruce Springsteen. And the rivalry between Naomi Campbell and Tyra Banks is legendary! Think about the people in your life who drive you crazy. Who are you the most competitive with? The answer will tell you everything you need to know about yourself. For me, it was Andy Cohen on Bravo. He had everything I thought I wanted. A dream job, chatting with cheeky reality stars while enjoying a cocktail in a club-like setting. As if that wasn't enough, Andy is best friends with my favorite little Miss *Sex and the City* herself, Sarah Jessica Parker! But the more I got to know Andy, the less I wanted to be like him. Conversely, the more I got to know about myself, the more I wanted to be like me. I realized that I was not competing with Andy Cohen, but rather using his success as an excuse to beat myself up. The only person I am competing with is me. Instead of focusing on him, I started to battle my own worries and self-doubts.

> *"The genuine truth, and I do think about this a lot, is that I'm one of the least competitive people you'll ever meet. Except with myself."*
> —Daniel Craig

There is more than enough room for us all to succeed. Instead of blaming others, take a look inward toward yourself. Instead of focusing on them, focus on you. And instead of being jealous, be inspired to make it happen for you. That's exactly what I did, and although I'm not yet besties with SJP, I do have my own daily podcast where I chat about all the cheeky reality stars while spilling the tea, and you better believe my apartment enjoys beautiful fresh flowers each week! Stop wallowing in self-pity and make a plan to turn that jealousy into action. When you become a fan of the person who once made you green with envy, you will become inspired. Observe them and their behavior to find out how they got what you want because at the end of the day, we are all the same. We are all human!

> *"A squirrel is just a rat with a cuter outfit."*
> —Sarah Jessica Parker

What Drives You?

When getting to know yourself, one of the most important things to learn is what motivates and drives you. Take a look at your daily life, your everyday routine, and ask, "What propels me?" What pushes you forward through the good and bad times, and what are you passionate about? Once you identify these motivations, you will hold a magic key that will unlock why you make the decisions you do. Instead of endlessly running through life, not knowing where you are going, for no reason other than just achieving more and more and more, stop to discover what is driving you and why.

> *"I think the first half of my 20s, I felt I had to achieve, achieve, achieve. A lot of men do this. I'm looking around now and I'm like, Where am I running?"*
> —Justin Timberlake

I saw you in NYC, and I almost didn't stop to say hello because, ironically, you looked like you were in a hurry, but I'm sure glad I did. That 6-minute conversation on the street was everything to me. I spent the entire trip home on the train thinking about what you said about discovering what drives me. I'm GOING THROUGH A DIVORCE and so consumed by that, I let revenge drive me. I had forgotten the great things in life, like my daughters and my friends. I don't want my kids to see Mom consumed by hate anymore. You're a huge inspiration to me. So thank you. —Anonymous

Think about the parts of your life that are the most important to you. The events, the activities, the simple quiet things you love to do, and the complicated loud moments that you can't live without. Take note of all the wonderful experiences you would miss dearly if they all suddenly disappeared and consider what they all have in common. Are they centered around your desire to be the best? Are you motivated by obtaining power and money? Are recognition and fame the driving factors behind what you do? Is it something entirely different? The key is to identify your motivations, and then, you will be able to identify you.

"Identity is a prison you can never escape, but the way to redeem your past is not to run from it, but to try to understand it, and use it as a foundation to grow."

—Jay Z

A lot of people are driven by their jobs, money, and income. Money is a very important motivating factor in everyone's life, and anyone who says it isn't does not know what it is like to not have enough. Without money, it would be impossible to live in this world; however, allowing money to become the single most important driving force in your life is a big mistake as money alone will not lead you to success and happiness. Make sure that you are running your business, rather than letting your business run you. Be aware that far too often greed takes over, to the point where gaining money becomes your main passion, rather than enjoying all the wonderful things money allows you to do.

> *"Being the richest man in the cemetery doesn't matter to me.... Going to bed at night saying we've done something wonderful... that's what matters to me."*
>
> —Steve Jobs

For me, money is now something that allows me to do the things I love. Growing up in a working-class family outside Birmingham, England, where I was the youngest of five children, I had no idea that my large family struggled so much that my dad had to take on a second job fitting carpets just to make ends meet. With a childhood full of love, laughter, and family, I always felt rich in the things that drove us. I had lots of fish and chips to eat, a cool Madonna-themed bedroom that I shared with my even cooler older brother, Douglas, and all five of us got a new pair of shoes each year to begin school. Yet even with this foundation of love, I later fell into the money trap. For a long period of time, all I was passionate about was the amount of money in my Chase bank account. Making money became the job itself. Until one day, I woke up with more money than I needed, and no one around to share it with. I could afford to buy my own fish and chips shop, enough new shoes to start each day with, front-row concert tickets to see Madonna in person, a home with so many bedrooms that I would never need to share again, and I still had enough money left over to get my cool older brother Douglas his own house, too. Yet, I had never been more miserable in my life.

"What are you going to do if you have all the money in the world and all the things that you wanted to achieve in your business, and you have no one to share it with? You come home alone at the end of the day. And then what?"

—Heidi Klum

Good morning! I wanted to let you know that I use The 4 Word Answer every morning. My alarm goes off at 6:30 AM, and before I leave for work, I make sure I kiss my wife and my kids and tell them that I love then. It reminds me why I'm working so hard. To think, before The Answer, I almost lost them all. I practically slept in that office and missed so many magical moments [in order] to earn more money. Just wanted to say thanks for reminding me what money is really about. —Jim

Just like money, the drive to be famous can take over your life. There are two types of famous people. There are the extraordinary, talented people with God-given gifts and expertise who did the work, found success, and got pushed into the spotlight.

These people didn't seek attention, but rather received it as a consequence of what they did. Then, there are the folks who don't do very much at all but desperately want to be famous for no other reason than the need for constant attention and approval. Fame itself is not the problem; it is why you are famous that is! Those driven by the endless need for reaffirmation always end in an ugly crash. This type of fame is fleeting and frivolous and will be forgotten very quickly, just as soon as the next train wreck comes along. Unfortunately, by then, you are already addicted to the dangerous drug called fame, which never fills the bottomless pit inside. All the attention in the outside world will never be enough to solve a problem that originates from deep within. In fact, fame only makes it worse.

> *"I want to poke holes in the erroneous beliefs about what fame provides. It won't raise your self-esteem, it won't create profound connection, it's not going to heal your childhood traumas, it's only going to amplify them. You're going to be subject to a lot of criticism and praise, both of which are violent in their own ways."*
>
> —Alanis Morrissette

By definition, leadership roles come with great power and influence over people's lives. It is a position of authority that should never be forgotten or taken for granted, but rather seen as a tool to be used to change the world, not control it. Most business leaders, bosses, and politicians work incredibly hard to get to the top of their profession. They are driven by a passion to make the world a better place; however, some steal their power by lying and cheating to obtain influence. Make sure that the power and influence you have in your life have been earned because power obtained in any other way is not power, it is abuse! When power and influence are only a means to an end, they become the end in itself. The people who want power because they feel weak will ultimately feel even weaker. Those trying to fool you into believing they are being selfless and benevolent as they strive for more and more power are, in fact, typically corrupt and selfish and always have a sad ending. The only way to gain real power and influence is to do the work and gain respect, because true power and influence can only be given not taken!

> *"My parents raised me to never feel like I was entitled to success, that you have to work for it. You have to work so hard for it. And sometimes you don't even get to where you need to go."*
> —Taylor Swift

Recognition is another major factor that people are very passionate about. It feels great when someone takes an interest and acknowledges you. Feeling recognized and valued is so important, especially in a world where it is way too easy to feel invisible and unimportant. Being ignored is awful and feeling lonely can happen anywhere to anyone—at work, at school, at a bar, and even at home. When you are not seen and not heard, it feels like your very existence doesn't matter at all, destroying whatever confidence and self-identity you have left. This is why it is only natural to want to be recognized.

> *"There is only one thing in life worse than being talked about, and that is not being talked about."*
> —Oscar Wilde

> *I listened to your podcast, and it was truly inspiring! I was so terrified of what people might say about me, I always tried to blend in and disappear. When you said the more successful you become, the haters come out, a bell went off. I wasn't scared of what other people said. I was scared of success and using them as an excuse. No more. Let them all talk about me. [It] shows that I must be doing something right. —Stephen*

What makes the drive of recognition so dangerous is that even those who receive attention for the right reasons can change and become obsessed with the need for validation. Crossing the line from enjoying a healthy amount of attention to becoming consumed by it will result in you surrendering and losing sight of who you are in exchange for the approval of others. This is why recognition cannot be the main thing that drives you in your life. Let the work be your passion, from which praise and acknowledgment will come. Any other method, including acting like a fool, might be much easier than putting in the work, but in the long term, it will backfire because, at the end of the day, the only real recognition and validation that you ever needed were from yourself!

> *"I worked hard to be accepted by the fashion community in ways beyond my physical appearance. In no time, though, I found myself surrendering to the industry's approval process. I felt like I needed validation from everyone. As a result, I lost sight*

of myself and what it meant to be happy, what it meant to be successful."

—Cara Delevingne

The passion to be the best drives a lot of people; however, the only ones to truly succeed are the ones who understand that they are only competing with themselves. Don't focus on beating others, but rather concentrate on being the best you can be. When you are driven by understanding that the only person in the race who matters is you, you will never lose again! It is not and never has been about others or finishing first, but rather all about you and putting yourself first. Don't worry about knocking other people out of the competition because those who make it to the top of the mountain of success are not spending a single minute worrying about you.

> *"Competition whose motive is merely to compete, to drive some other fellow out, never carries very far. The competitor to be feared is one who never bothers about you at all, but goes on making his own business better all the time."*
>
> —Henry Ford

What drives me, especially as I grow, is having a purpose and fighting for a better tomorrow for all of us, which ironically has given me a better today. You don't get to spend as much time in a children's hospital as I did without leaving wanting to ease the pain of others, and truthfully, a little of your own pain, too. In the past, I have been driven by lots of different things—money, fame, power, influence, recognition, and even the need to beat other people. None of the motivations has ever driven me to a place of peace. What has is lending a helping hand to others. It has nothing to do with me trying to be a good person or even helping out those with less privilege, but rather everything to do with me finding my purpose, my passion, and finally feeling useful. The secret that very few people know is that when you are driven to help others, you end up helping yourself more.

> *"No one is useless in this world who lightens the burdens of another."*
>
> —Charles Dickens

Dear ROB — I just wanted to say thank you for saying what I needed to hear in a language that I could understand. For making me get off the couch and find my purpose. For getting me to follow my passions, and you are 100% right: when you help others you help yourself! —Alan

For years, I would be driven by avoiding sick people. Because of my accident, visiting people in the hospital was a traumatic experience for me. The sight of nurses in scrubs, the feel of plastic chairs in the waiting area, but most of all, the smell of the disinfection, all made me turn and run away. I wanted to get so far away that I couldn't be hurt again; however, identifying these feelings gave me the power to know myself and eventually change my behavior. Take the time to find out what drives everything you do. Be kind and nonjudgmental while you are searching because, I promise you, there will be plenty of time after you find out who you are! Now is the time for the truth and only the truth.

Your bright future is depending on it. Put the complicated jigsaw puzzle of your life together one piece at a time and reveal the big, beautiful picture of who you are and what passions drive you.

> *"Nothing is as important as passion. No matter what you want to do with your life, be passionate."*
> —Jon Bon Jovi

Get to Know Your Body

Getting to know your body is not easy because it brings up a whole bunch of judgments and emotions. This is why you have to commit to getting to know yourself and renew the commitment when the going gets tough. Think about it. You probably know the bodies of your favorite celebrities better than you know your own! It would be much easier to identify Kim Kardashian's bottom, Bradley Cooper's blue eyes, or Julia Roberts' big smile than picking out your own! Well, that stops today because we all need to start paying a lot more attention to ourselves and a lot less attention to others.

> *"Your body is not a temple, it's an amusement park. Enjoy the ride."*
> —Anthony Bourdain

Get rid of the notion that you would be happier if you had a different body. This is simply not true; it is a false narrative that we use as an excuse. What is true is that we are constantly being sold a lie—the lie that if we look a certain way, all our problems will go away. I have worked with people who are considered the most perfect in the world, including Tyra Banks, Naomi

Campbell, Molly Sims, and Petra Nemcova, representing and getting to know them. I can promise you that even they feel insecure and, on occasions, even ugly, too! Just look at all the eating disorders and drug addictions surrounding the fashion and entertainment business as proof. Erase the notion that if you looked different, your life would be movie-star happy.

> *"I thought, 'he [Jason Sudeikis] won't be interested in me; I'm not a contender.' He was so cool, so funny—I was such a fan of his and had always fancied his speed and his intelligence. I thought, 'I'm not beautiful enough or his type.'"*
>
> —Olivia Wilde

For years, I blamed everything that went wrong with my life on my bad skin. I didn't have a boyfriend because of my skin. I didn't get a promotion because I wasn't a pretty girl. My friends sucked because of the way I looked. Then, I met the most beautiful girl I had ever seen. She looked like Princess Diana, and just like Diana, her husband had left her for another woman! I realized that being gorgeous didn't solve all your problems. That has to come from the inside. I'm on new medicine now, and my skin has healed beautifully, but I still didn't get a promotion, boyfriend, or great friends, even with crystal clear skin, until I started to live The 4 Word Answer. It turns out the best look of all is knowing you are kind, important, smart and yourself. Love you! —Ruth

Take control of the messages you tell your brain. Instead of putting filters on your Instagram pictures, start putting filters on what you allow to get inside your head. Stop following celebrities and friends on social media just because they look good. Get rid of anyone in your life who makes you feel bad about the way you look. We all need to be much more careful with what people, images, and messages we internalize. It is a choice. You have the power to create boundaries around everything that does not empower you. Growing up, I didn't have anyone who looked like me. Disabled people were never in magazines, and the only ones on TV were victims, someone to feel sorry for or pity, and they would always be single. This sent me the clear message at a very early age that looking different meant I would always be alone. Thanks to technology, we can now curate more of what we consume. In this cruel world, make sure you surround yourself with people who make you feel beautiful. Make sure your life, both on social media and in reality, is packed with people who look like you, and get out there and represent!

> *"We never say, 'Who's going to be the next Matt Damon?' because there's George Clooney. We never say, 'Who's going to be the next George Clooney?' because there's Tom Hanks. We never say who's going to be the next (of) those people because there's an abundance, but when it comes to people of color, you'll see that there's normally just one or two and that's it."*
>
> —Mo'Nique

Before you can love your body, you have got to get to know it. The good news is that your body is communicating with you constantly; all you have to do is listen. Forget Tesla and Apple products. Every one of us already owns the most amazing custom-made machine ever made: our bodies! Take pride in getting to know how it works and all its functions, settings, and things it can do. Most people are only using a small percentage of what their body is capable of, a terrible waste considering it can do so much. Learn to use it to its full potential and get into the habit of doing something that makes it feel great—every single day. I've turned something as ordinary as brushing my teeth into a daily two-minute blissful routine! It is the only time when I am totally by myself—not even my puppy, Darby, comes into my bathroom. I unleash the soft sensation of the clean toothbrush inside my mouth, enjoying that heavenly tangy, two-minute peppermint sparkle burst twice a day! Find those little moments in your life, too. They might be weird, but who cares, as long as they make you feel good?

> *"I think everybody is weird. We should all cele-brate our individuality and not be embarrassed or ashamed of it."*
>
> —Johnny Depp

> *My body has been telling me that I needed to lose 60 lbs. for a decade, but I am an emotional eater and didn't listen until you spelled it out. Now, instead of reaching for junk food, I go for a walk when I get upset. After 5 months, I'm up to walking 2 miles a day, and I am amazed at the changes in my body and my mind. I have lost 45lbs, sleep better, breathe better and the clouds and fog in my head are gone. I have turned the simple act of walking, putting one foot in front of another, into the best part of my day. And I did it with just FOUR SIMPLE WORDS! Grateful, Doris*

Make the conscious choice to learn to love your body. It will take a little time before you fall head-over-heels, and as in all relationships, there will be a lot of ups and downs, some doubt, and even uncertainty along the way. It took me a while to get to this place, coming from a place where I wasn't just insecure about my right arm but also my weight. My size defined me for years, to the point where I actually thought about making an appointment to see a top plastic surgeon who one of my "perfect" model clients secretly saw! Despite all the great things I had going for me, all I could see and hear were people looking and talking about my weight, sending me running to the gym. When I wasn't working out, I was staying home, starving myself trying to get their approval. Until I gave in and called the doctor with lots of celebrity clients and went under the knife. Post-surgery and many pounds lighter, I had never been more miserable in my life. Quickly I gained back all the weight and then some, too. It wasn't until I discovered *The 4 Word Answer* that I finally lost sixty pounds and kept it off. I am happier and healthier than ever and no longer living at the gym or running to the doctor's office anymore. And this time, I did it for me!

Have you ever looked at a picture of yourself and not liked the person staring back? I used to hate looking at pictures I was in, so shocked by what I saw that I couldn't believe it was me! I would gasp, seeing only my big nose, double chin, lazy eye, and broken arm. Then, around the time of the US Open in New York, I was invited to a super fancy tennis party hosted by Rafael Nadal. I'm not a huge sports fan, but I've always had a little crush on Roger Federer. His dark beady eyes that are so close together they would touch if it wasn't for his big handsome Roman nose keeping them apart! Standing outside on the terrace of the Empire Hotel, a young guest came over to me and asked, "Excuse me, can I take a picture with you?" "Sure," I replied as I screamed internally, "I hate taking photos. I always take bad pictures! It won't even look like me!" It wasn't totally unheard of for strangers to occasionally recognize me from TV and ask for a picture together. I assumed this super hip young lady was more of a *Wendy Williams Show* watcher than CNN! To my surprise, she was neither. She didn't care about Wendy and Anderson Cooper at all. In fact, the only person she cared about was Mr.! Roger! Federer! Which was exactly who she thought I was! This cool lady, with obvious great taste, thought I was my straight crush! Before I could reveal the truth, she was gone! But not before leaving me an amazing lesson. If someone I didn't know could see me as handsome, then why couldn't I be kind enough to see it myself?

> *"Sometimes it takes only one act of kindness and caring to change a person's life."*
> —Jackie Chan

The reason I couldn't see it was that I didn't know what I looked like. All our eyes look outward toward other people, not back at ourselves. We all spend far more time looking at everyone else rather than at ourselves, simply because of the way we have been designed. This is why so many of us, including me, are surprised and shocked when we finally get a good look at our faces. And this is why mirror work is so important. Not just glancing at yourself twice a day when you are brushing your teeth and having a lovely moment. No, we all need to become experts in the intense work of standing in front of a mirror for an extended period of time to study and learn to know the face looking back. Really looking at yourself is one of the most direct and dynamic ways to uncover the truth, and the most effective way to do this is to stand in front of a mirror every day, sometimes naked!

"I had to fight, a lot of years, to be really proud of the person I see in the mirror and really love this person."
—Jonathan Van Ness

My relationship with myself has improved 1000% since I started 'mirror work.' At first it felt silly, and all I could see were the faults, like the first time you walk into someone's house and spot all the flaws. But after a while, I didn't notice the little things anymore. Over time, I have come to love it. I might never be commercially beautiful, but I'm not a bad-looking person at all. Now I find great comfort seeing that special friend I know very well looking back at me instead of a stranger. Thanks, Rob —Tammy

Stand there in front of the mirror until you have something kind to say. You just have to find one nice thing to focus on. Maybe it's your hands, your smile, those bright eyes, or those great legs you haven't looked at in years? Learn to replace the cruel habit of self-shaming with the kind routine of self-love. Stand there and don't move until you stop beating yourself up. Because once you find that one small thing about yourself that you like, you will start to notice another and another and another. All it takes is a little practice. Refuse to give up on yourself, and you will not only learn to accept the way you look, but you will also learn to love it.

> *"I used to look in the mirror and feel shame, I look in the mirror now and I absolutely love myself."*
> —Drew Barrymore

Now whenever your brain starts complaining about your body, stop and remind yourself of all the things you like. I have accepted that I will never have six-pack abs, but I do have fantastic thick hair. I'm never going to weigh less than 200 pounds, but I am always going to be tall! Choose to dwell on your strengths, to focus on what you like. After all, you have been beating yourself up because of the way you look for years, and that hasn't worked out so well for you! Be kind to yourself and take the time to learn about your body. The more you know, the more it will amaze you. Now look straight into the mirror and say out loud, "You is (add your name)."

> *"You have to stand up and say, 'There's nothing wrong with me or my shape or who I am, you're the one with the problem!'"*
> —Jennifer Lopez

C
H
A
P
T
E
R

The Answer Was Just Four Words Away All Along

THE ONLY THING YOU EVER NEEDED WAS TO BELIEVE IN THE power of words—specifically four words! You are **kind**, you are **smart**, you are **important**, and you are **you**!

I can't remember how many times a day I needed to remind myself that I was all four when I first discovered *The 4 Word Answer*. But now, after just a few years of continuous use, all I need is four seconds every morning and four seconds every evening to know who I am.

> *"Continuous effort—not strength or intelligence—is the key to unlocking our potential."*
> —Winston Churchill

Right at the beginning of our adventure, long before I name-dropped all those celebrities, I warned you that *The 4 Word Answer* might sound silly at first. It certainly did to me when it first appeared in my life. Now, there is not a single thing that I am more serious about. Nothing has proven to work or has been more consistent in providing me with the answer to every single question, other than *The 4 Word Answer*! Now, after showing that it has worked its magic for me, celebrities, and hundreds of thousands of people around the world, it is time that *The 4 Word Answer* started working for you. The life you were always meant to live is just four words away. Now that you know what those four words are, the only thing left to do is to find the strength and courage to forgive the past!

> *"The weak can never forgive. Forgiveness is the attribute of the strong."*
>
> —Mahatma Gandhi

Forgive Yourself

Change your relationship with the past, and you will change your relationship with the future. A bright tomorrow requires that you deal with the dark wounds from yesterday, right now. The key to opening the door to everything you ever wanted is *The 4 Word Answer*, and forgiveness is the lock. When they work together, the Tiffany Blue door, or whatever color door you want, will swing open to your freedom.

"As I walked out the door toward the gate that would lead to my freedom, I knew if I didn't leave my bitterness and hatred behind, I'd still be in prison."

—Nelson Mandela

When you no longer loathe your past, you will no longer loathe your future. In fact, the only thing a bad past is good for is preparing to have a great tomorrow. I know it is much easier said than done. Change is hard, and forgiveness is even harder. Yet, when you choose to forgive, you always end up helping yourself much more than those who wronged you. You have been beating yourself up for far too long, hoping to hurt others, when in reality, you have only been hurting yourself. It is time to try something new. It is time to forgive and even be grateful for everything that has happened to you!

"True forgiveness is when you can say 'Thank you for that experience.'"

—Oprah Winfrey

Pain hides beneath every wound. Until you have forgiven, it is only a scab away from being exposed again. It takes time to heal, which is why you don't have another minute to lose. Make sure that when you are ready to forgive, you are truly forgiving, because pretending to forgive won't cure anything at all. True forgiveness is when you truly forgive yourself. It has to start and end with you. Only when you love yourself again today can you escape the hate of your past.

> *"Darkness cannot drive out darkness; only light*
> *can do that. Hate cannot drive out hate; only love*
> *can do that."*
> —Martin Luther King Jr.

Just a few days ago, I failed miserably! A new doorman in my building accidentally misplaced a package that I had convinced myself was a matter of life or death—which, of course, it wasn't. I wasn't kind, I wasn't smart, I wasn't important, and I was not myself! After all these years, I didn't think I would ever see that guy again. It took me a moment, or more precisely, it took me four seconds to remind myself that I am kind, smart, important, and me, and it worked. The real Rob was back! I took responsibility, apologized, and promised that I would do better. The specifics of my behavior do not matter. What does matter is that we all make mistakes, and when we do, we must admit it. It takes courage to admit you were wrong, but it takes even more courage to forgive yourself and make it right.

> *"Mistakes are always forgivable, if one has the*
> *courage to admit them."*
> —Bruce Lee

We all have shameful episodes when our better angels gave in to our darkest impulses, but continuing to obsess and beat yourself up doesn't help. While you can't go back in time and get a do-over, you can move forward by forgiving yourself and recommitting to making different choices in the future. Forgiveness leaves you able to focus on doing great tomorrow instead of reliving the bad decisions from the past.

"Forgiveness is a gift you give yourself."
—Tony Robbins

We are all works in progress, making our way along the complicated path of life. Mistakes will be made, mistakes that you will learn to be grateful for. However, the biggest mistake you could ever make is getting stuck. Keep moving forward, one new step and thought at a time. Don't worry, there will be plenty more mistakes to make as the journey continues (wink), but you have to keep going. Remember, once you forgive, you are no longer your yesterday. Once you forgive, you are no longer your tomorrow. Once you forgive, you are your right now!

"Yesterday is gone. Tomorrow has not yet come. We have only today. Let us begin."
—Mother Theresa

Don't Hold Grudges

There have been so many delicious celebrity feuds over the years: Madonna and Elton John, Jennifer Aniston and Angelina Jolie and who could ever forget Rosie O'Donnell and Donald Trump? However, my favorite celebrity feud of all time is the one between Taylor Swift and Katy Perry. It all began back in 2013 when a dancer left Taylor's show to join Katy's. Skip forward a year, and Taylor tells *Rolling Stone* magazine, no less, that her new song is about an artist who "tried to sabotage" her tour! Add to all that the fact that both ladies were connected with serial celebrity dater, John Mayer, and a bunch of cryptic tweets referencing Rachel McAdams' character in *Mean Girls*, and you are in *Us*

Weekly heaven! The reason that this is my all-time favorite celebrity feud is not because of what happened, but rather because of how it ended. Just when we had almost forgotten why these two ever fell out in the first place, Katy extended an olive branch. Yes, Katy Perry literally sent Taylor Swift an actual branch from an olive tree, to which Taylor responded with a platter of chocolate chip cookies with the words, *"PEACE AT LAST,"* written in icing on top!

Now, we might not have access to an actual olive tree, but we do all have access to colleagues, friends, lovers, and even family members who have left a bitter taste in our mouths. Take a leaf out of Katy's book and realize that letting go of a grudge has nothing to do with the person who wronged you. Rather, letting go of a grudge has everything to do with the person who was wronged: you! Don't forgive because they deserve it, forgive them because you deserve it. We are never totally blameless. When you recognize this, you can reframe your grudge as an opportunity to forgive, because putting down the poison you have been drinking or the heavy load of hate you have been carrying is the ultimate act of self-love.

> *"It's not an easy journey, to get to a place where you forgive people. But it is such a powerful place, because it frees you."*
>
> —Tyler Perry

Before *The 4 Word Answer*, I would hold on to a grudge for so long that it became my identity. Having convinced myself that because I was the victim of unforgivable deeds, I was trapped in my unforgettable past. However, the truth was, it wasn't that I couldn't move on. It was that I didn't want to move on. I became so comfortable wearing the label of being "wronged" that it was a badge of honor. It fit me like a fine tailored Brooks Brothers tuxedo that I didn't want to ever take off. Showing off my injuries made me feel deserving of the sympathy I didn't receive at the time of the crime. Yet, basking in the wrongs of my past made it impossible to be free to participate in my rights of tomorrow.

When your grudge becomes your main story, it also becomes your main obstacle to healing. Instead of looking for empathy everywhere you go, be the one who gives it...even to that naughty sister! Take back the responsibility for caring about your own suffering, something that is far too important to ever be trusted to anyone else, and give yourself kindness that you were never shown. Holding on to a grudge neither heals you nor hurts others. It is only when you are able to forgive that you are able to find the compassion that you crave. Focus on today, rather than being consumed by the past. The happier you are right now, the more you will be able to forgive what happened back then. The more you are able to forgive, the happier you will be!

> *"When you are happy, you can forgive a great deal."*
> —Princess Diana

Now You Know You Are Kind

Think of how much you will be able to achieve by choosing to be kind. Turning down the volume of that cruel voice in your head might not make you the next Paul McCartney, but it will make you the best version of you. The next time that ugly lie gets a little too loud, "Sarah Palin" it away. Thinking about the most average people who have achieved the most extraordinary success will always make you feel "good enough!" Enjoy every single bite of your new delicious "attention diet," knowing you will never be hungry again for anyone else's permission. Keep devouring all the good people you can while cutting out all the bad apples from your daily diet. Remember, when they can't be kind, they have to go.

You will notice very quickly that choosing to see life through positive eyes changes the way you see everything. The simple adjustment of asking, "What happened?" instead of, "What's wrong?" will reveal all. It is worth repeating; there is absolutely *nothing* wrong with you, except the way you once thought about yourself! Remember that kindness attracts kindness and that kindness starts with you. You have planted the seeds that will now grow into the most beautiful flowering garden of friendship. There will be no room for any more weeds now that your life is jam-packed with gorgeous blooms that you shower with kindness like it is manure! Go on, pull out your phone right now and text yourself something kind. We will wait!

Don't forget that if you are choosing it, you are changing it. Choose to be kind, because when you change your decisions, you change your life.

> *"No one is kinder to themselves than celebrities, so treat yourself like the star you were always meant to be."*
>
> —Rob Shuter

Now You Know You Are Smart

Doesn't it feel great to admit that we all need a little help? It took the smartest person I have ever met, Jessica Simpson, to teach me that. She will love that I am now passing it on to you. Because the only real chance any of us have is when we are smart enough to keep trying. No one has failed more times than our very own Angela—to use her secret name! But every time she gets knocked down, she gets back up and tries again. Smart people always choose courage over comfort, so let me be the first to wish you a very long future of always getting back up...and ultimately succeeding!

Like you, I misdiagnosed myself for years as being lazy. It wasn't until *The 4 Word Answer* that I found out I wasn't lazy at all—I was scared. I was full of fear and constantly frightened of failing. All that changed when I started to play the "positive mind game." I chose to think about winning, not losing, and when I decided to think this and not that, even daily tasks, like walking Darby, were different! The small decisions you make each day quickly add up to define the big picture of your life, so start making smart ones that come from a place of yes.

I started *The 4 Word Answer* after being inspired by a movie; however, I finished *The 4 Word Answer* after I did the work every single day. Be smart enough to focus on the next four minutes, and the next four years take care of themselves.

> *"It is smart to be kind, and it is kind to know that you are smart."*
>
> —Rob Shuter

Now You Know You Are Important

I didn't know it at the time, but Diane Sawyer gave me the most important advice on our flight to Prague. The way you treat people reveals everything about you, so treat everyone like they are important. Sooner rather than later, that person you make feel important today is going to play an important role in your life tomorrow. Know that you possess the same fairy dust as Puff the Magic Dragon, so use it! Sprinkle it over every relationship in your life, including the most important relationship you are ever going to have: the one with yourself. Fill life so full of respect and love that there won't be any room left for anyone who doesn't make you feel important. Surround yourself with people who always send you home with a big fat smile on your face, even though you don't need anyone else's approval but your own.

The more important the dream, the more time it takes to make it come true, so don't forget why you started. The beginning is always more important than the end, which is why a strong foundation, a lot of hard work, and a little help from *The 4 Word Answer* will mean you cannot fail. Effort is the only currency success accepts. Show up one more time than the others who quit. Remember you don't "have to" do this, you "get to" do it. If a young kid with a lisp and a big gap between his two front teeth learned to believe he is important, then so can you.

> *"Making everyone, including yourself, know that they are important isn't just the kind thing to do, it is the smart thing to do."*
>
> —Rob Shuter

Now You Know You Are...(insert your name)

Knowing who you are will make you a star in your life. We were all born as strangers, making life a journey of discovery. Find the courage to know everything you can about yourself. True love's kiss can only come from you, and once you wake up to the truth about who you are, all your dreams will come true. Knowing what you like and dislike is not the same as knowing what is popular and unpopular. Knowing what you believe and value is not the same as adopting the values and beliefs of someone else. Don't be afraid to be you; be afraid of trying to be someone else.

Surround yourself with the hobbies and passions you love. If Taylor Swift can still find time to build a snow globe, then you can find time to embrace your passions. Discover the folks who care about the same things you do. Find a way to be part of that world—even if it means starting out selling ice cream! Don't be jealous of people who have what you want; be inspired by them. When I stopped using Andy Cohen's success as an excuse to beat myself up about the lack of my achievements, I started competing with the only person who ever mattered—me!

The 4 Word Answer will impact every single relationship in your life, including the important one you have with your body. No longer know the bodies of celebrities better than you know your own. Pretending to be invisible doesn't make you disappear. It is time to stop running away from what you look like and start running toward the mirror. I promise it does get easier to see the truth when you know you are kind, smart, and important. It took the eyes of a tennis-loving stranger for me to start seeing myself; however, it was *The 4 Word Answer* that opened up my eyes, heart, and brain.

Only after I got to know myself did the old burns from the boiler room of celebrity heal. Only after I accepted myself did I stop trying to hide my right arm in shame. And only after I started to love myself did I finally believe my dear friend Kate Spade: I was "practically perfect in every way."

> *"It is smart to be kind. It is kind to be smart. And it's both smart and kind to believe that everyone, especially you, is important."*
>
> —Rob Shuter

* * *

Just like Dorothy Gale, who needed to fly over the rainbow and back, you too needed to get to the end of our story to realize that all the answers you ever needed were already inside you. You are, and you always have been, *the answer*. As the Wizard himself declared, "Everything you were looking for was right there with you all along!"

When we first started out together, all those pages ago, you can now admit that you might have thought *The 4 Word Answer* sounded a little crazy! I will confess, I thought the same thing when it first appeared in my life. Now we both know that the only crazy thing about the answer is that no one ever told us there was a question before! Thankfully, the secret is finally out of the bag, or the book, and now no matter how distant the solution may seem, the answer is just four words away. The trick is to not wait until you next need it, but rather to take the preventive medicine every day—with or without a spoonful of sugar. I can't promise you that *The 4 Word Answer* will transform you into the "perfect" person, or that your partner will no longer leave dirty dishes in the sink, but I can promise that you will now be the person you were always meant to be. I still have those yellow Post-its taped to my computer screen at home, but now they no longer belong to Jennifer Lopez, Diddy, Alicia Keys, or Jessica Simpson. Now they belong to me. One word per Post-it, four Post-its per Rob!

That annoyingly happy English chap who came to America with his trumpet and his master's degree (did I mention he has a master's degree?) is back; however, as proud as I am of graduating from the University of Edinburgh, my real education came from Professor Simpson, Professor Keys, Professor Lopez, Professor Banks, Professor Campbell, Professor Bon Jovi, and my favorite, Professor Diddy. Allowing a working-class kid from the Midlands, who didn't know his Dolce from his Gabbana, to get to know you changed my life completely and ultimately allowed me to get to know me. I will always be eternally grateful to each and every one of you, and to all the other people whose names I have been constantly dropping! I know for a fact some of you were worried when the news broke in the press that I was writing a book, but I told you that you didn't have anything to worry about…. I'm saving all the scandalous stuff for the next one (wink)!

Now *The 4 Word Answer* belongs to you. It is as much yours as it is mine, or the hundreds of thousands of people whose lives it has already changed. No more quotes from Oprah, Jennifer Lopez, Alicia Keys, Claire from Texas, or even me. Now it's time for you to tell your story. And so, the last quote in the book has to belong to you. Don't worry, no pressure: it's been on the tip of your tongue all along. All you needed was a little help from a friend to let you know it was there!

> *"I am kind. I am smart. I am important. I am (add your name)."*
>
> —You!

About the Author

Called "America's Number ONE Gossip Columnist" by *The National Enquirer*, Rob "Naughty But Nice" Shuter breaks celebrity news every day on his website NaughtyGossip.com, where he delivers all the dish about the stars we love in his naughty but nice signature style. You can also catch him co-hosting and breaking celebrity news on *Good Day New York*, the *Today* show, *The Talk*, *The Wendy Williams Show*, CNN, *Extra*, and Z100's *Elvis Duran*. Previously, Rob was the *Huffington Post*'s only celebrity columnist and the former executive editor of *OK!* magazine. Rob has also hosted his own Saturday night talk show on Mark Cuban's channel and his own daily morning show, *The Gossip Table*, on VH1. Breaking some of the biggest entertainment stories, including Jamie Lynn Spears' pregnancy news, Britney's first post-meltdown interview, Eva Longoria's wedding, and baby exclusives for Jessica Alba, Tori Spelling, and Matthew McConaughey's tots, Rob always knows where to find the best scoop. Before Rob was one of the world's most successful entertainment reporters, he was a publicist working for Jennifer Lopez, Alicia Keys, P. Diddy, Jessica Simpson, and Jon Bon Jovi! Now he is bringing all this experience to his new show on iHeartMedia in his unique cheeky way: always a pinch and never a punch!